ROUTLEDGE LIBRARY EDITIONS:
BUSINESS CYCLES

Volume 4

T0316056

THREE ESSAYS ON PRODUCTIVITY

THREE ESSAYS ON PRODUCTIVITY
The Impacts of Profitability, Business Cycles and the Capital Stock on Productivity

MARK J. LASKY

Routledge
Taylor & Francis Group

LONDON AND NEW YORK

First published in 1994

This edition first published in 2015
by Routledge
2 Park Square, Milton Park, Abingdon, Oxon, OX14 4RN

and by Routledge
711 Third Avenue, New York, NY 10017

Routledge is an imprint of the Taylor & Francis Group, an informa business

British Library Cataloguing in Publication Data
A catalogue record for this book is available from the British Library

ISBN: 978-1-138-85286-0 (Set)
eISBN: 978-1-315-71360-1 (Set)
ISBN: 978-1-138-86107-7 (Volume 4)
eISBN: 978-1-315-71494-3 (Volume 4)
Pb ISBN: 978-1-138-88628-5 (Volume 4)

Publisher's Note
The publisher has gone to great lengths to ensure the quality of this reprint but points out that some imperfections in the original copies may be apparent.

Disclaimer
The publisher has made every effort to trace copyright holders and would welcome correspondence from those they have been unable to trace.

THREE ESSAYS ON PRODUCTIVITY

THE IMPACTS OF PROFITABILITY, BUSINESS CYCLES AND THE CAPITAL STOCK ON PRODUCTIVITY

MARK J. LASKY

GARLAND PUBLISHING, INC.
NEW YORK & LONDON / 1994

Library of Congress Cataloging-in-Publication Data

Lasky, Mark J., 1960–
 Three essays on productivity : the impacts of profitability, business
cycles and the capital stock on productivity / Mark J. Lasky.
  p.   cm. — (Garland studies on industrial productivity)
 An outgrowth of the author's doctoral dissertation in economics
completed in 1991 at Massachusetts Institute of Technology.
 Includes bibliographical references and index.
 ISBN 0–8153–1622–4 (alk. paper)
 1. Production (Economic theory).   2. Industrial productivity.
3. Profit. 4. Business cycles. 5. Capital productivity.   I. Title.
II. Series.
HB241.L36   1994
338.5—dc20   93–48968
                                                            CIP

Printed on acid-free, 250-year-life paper
Manufactured in the United States of America

To my parents

CONTENTS

TABLES

CHARTS

PREFACE

This book began as my doctoral dissertation in economics at the Massachusetts Institute of Technology. The first essay (chapter) of the book started as a study of the relationship between profits, wages, prices and productivity over the business cycle. Based on visual inspection of U.S. postwar data, it appeared that productivity growth is stronger when profits' share of GNP has been low in prior years, and weaker when profits have been strong. Although at first I thought this might be a key to explaining the business cycle, further study revealed that the impact of profits on productivity does not depend on the stage of the business cycle. Rather, it may help to explain such non-cyclical phenomena as the acceleration in manufacturing productivity growth in the 1980s, when profits were held down by foreign competition.

The behavior of U.S. productivity since my dissertation was completed in early 1991 has added new relevance to this relationship between profits and productivity. While some observers have hailed the sharp acceleration in productivity growth since 1990 as the beginning of a new era of higher productivity growth, others have argued that the acceleration is normal cyclical behavior. Given the unusually low level of profits in 1990-91, I add a third possibility: the portion of the acceleration in productivity growth in excess of normal cyclical behavior has been caused by efforts to restore profitability, and will thus fade once profitability has been restored. The surprising drop in productivity during the first half of 1993 may provide some evidence for this hypothesis.

The second and third chapters each began as efforts to find alternative explanations for surprising empirical results obtained by other researchers: Robert Hall's estimates of large markups of price over marginal cost, and Paul Romer's finding that output is much more dependent on capital than on labor in the long run. Thus, the second chapter shows that Hall's estimates of price over marginal cost are biased up, while the third chapter shows that freely estimated production functions should not be used to measure the impact of capital on output. Possibly because of the problems inherent in this estimation technique, recent research on the importance of capital in the production function—notably that of De Long, Summers, and

Wolff—has emphasized the relationship between investment and output growth, at least partially solving the problem.

I am greatly indebted to my professors and colleagues at M.I.T. for their help and advice. Ernst Berndt provided many insightful comments, especially on the second essay, and was a source of encouragement throughout. Stanley Fischer guided the work as it first took shape. Roland Benabou then added rigor to the economic models and helped curb my tendency to add extraneous digressions to the text. Olivier Blanchard offered several helpful suggestions.

Robert Hall provided data used in the regressions of the second chapter. I have made use of the computer and data facilities of both M.I.T. and DRI/McGraw-Hill. Thomas Piccone provided computer assistance and Dale Lasky (my father) helped proofread the manuscript.

I am deeply grateful for the support and encouragement of friends and colleagues too numerous to mention in this space. Without them, this book would not have been possible. I owe a great deal to my parents, who taught me to set high standards for myself and to achieve them. And I thank God, who makes all things possible.

INTRODUCTION

Productivity is intimately connected with both the long run and short run performance of the economy. In the long run, productivity growth determines the economic standard of living. For example, if labor productivity (output per labor hour) were to grow at the 2.51% annual rate averaged from 1947 to 1973, living standards would double every 28 years, while if productivity grew at the 0.88% annual rate averaged from 1973 to 1992, it would take 79 years for living standards to double. In the short run, productivity determines the relationship between output and jobs. For example, holding output and the average workweek constant, an extra percentage point of labor productivity growth means one less percentage point of job growth. This book consists of three essays (chapters) examining the impact of profits, the business cycle, and the capital stock on productivity.

The basis of the first chapter is the empirical finding that, controlling for normal business cycle effects, productivity grows faster when profits have been low than otherwise. The remainder of the chapter investigates possible explanations for this behavior. The one that appears most consistent with the data is that low profits, by triggering fear of bankruptcy or plant shutdown, stimulate efforts by workers and managers to improve productivity.

It is important to realize that the negative response of productivity to profits at the fairly short term frequencies examined in this study does not preclude a positive impact of profits or the profit motive on productivity in the longer run. Rather, the profits-productivity relationship appears useful in explaining the behavior of productivity growth during episodes such as the slowdown and subsequent acceleration of productivity growth in 1988-92. It also suggests that policies which boost profits by reducing competitive pressure, such as protectionist trade measures, may hurt productivity growth.

The second chapter discusses how to measure marginal cost using time series data. The intuitive approach—to divide output minus trend productivity growth by growth in inputs—is shown to fail, because some of the marginal cost of current changes in output occurs in later periods. I show that to correctly estimate marginal cost, one must account for the change in costs which is deferred to the future—"deferred marginal cost"—as well as the portion of the current change in costs which reflects lagged adjustment to past output changes. Studies that fail to account for deferred marginal cost will produce estimates of marginal cost which are too low.

Implicitly, such a discussion of the relationship between output and labor costs is a discussion of productivity. Indeed, the second chapter of this book shows how deferred marginal cost, combined with profit-maximizing firms and utility-maximizing workers, can generate procyclical productivity. Such a causal link from output to productivity reverses the direction of causality found in the real business cycle literature, in which changes in productivity lead to changes in output.

The third chapter tests a basic assumption of the first two chapters: the assumption that productivity growth is exogenous to labor and capital. I show that one technique recently used to test this assumption—simply regressing output on labor hours, the capital stock, and a constant—provides a misleading estimate of the impact of capital on output. If multifactor productivity grows at the same rate in the capital-producing sector as in the rest of the economy, then the ratio of wages to the cost of capital, which determines the capital-labor ratio, will vary positively with multifactor productivity. Thus, in the simple regression mentioned above, the capital stock will proxy for multifactor productivity, and will receive too large a coefficient. Adding relative factor prices can correct for this bias.

Three Essays on Productivity

I.

Do Low Profits Stimulate Productivity Growth?

1. INTRODUCTION

Why did productivity grow so rapidly in 1991-92, after declining over the prior three years? Following a 0.5% drop from the fourth quarter of 1987 to the fourth quarter of 1990, output per hour worked in the nonfarm business sector grew 2.3% over the next four quarters and 3.7% during 1992, the largest four-quarter increase since the mid 1970s. Certainly part of the explanation is that productivity is procyclical, and real GDP growth accelerated between the two periods. The surge in productivity during 1992, however, was larger than one would normally expect given the modest rate of growth of real output.[1]

Many observers have hailed this development as evidence of a new era of more rapid productivity growth. (Robert Gordon provided a good summary.)[2] The flip side of this rapid productivity growth, however, has been the snail's pace of job creation: the growth rate of total hours worked equals the rate of growth of output minus the growth rate of productivity (output per hour), so more rapid productivity growth, given output growth, means slower growth in hours, and thus in employment. Observers have also been warning of a new era of slow job growth.

One frequently cited explanation for the 1991-92 acceleration in productivity growth is a shift from labor to capital, possibly due to a decline in the cost of capital relative to the cost of labor. However, this theory performs poorly over the period in question—capital investment per dollar of GDP and labor productivity actually moved in opposite directions over the period 1987-93 (Chart 1.1). It appears that at the

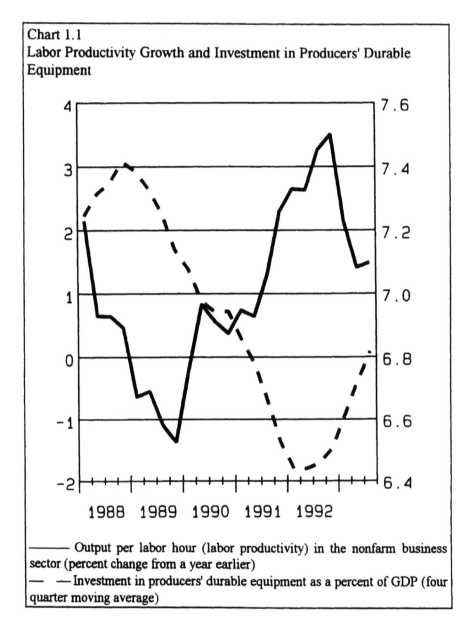

Chart 1.1
Labor Productivity Growth and Investment in Producers' Durable Equipment

——— Output per labor hour (labor productivity) in the nonfarm business sector (percent change from a year earlier)
— —Investment in producers' durable equipment as a percent of GDP (four quarter moving average)

same time businesses were boosting output per worker, they were also boosting output per unit of capital. Some other explanation must be found for the unusual behavior of productivity growth during this period than higher investment.

One of the most vexing problems in economics since the late 1970s has been finding an explanation for the productivity slowdown that began sometime during the prior ten years. In an exhaustive study, Edward Denison proposed 17 different possible explanations for the slowdown, but was able to reject each one.[3] Norsworthy, Harper and Kunze, using a different treatment of the business cycle, were able to explain the 1973-79 slowdown as the result of a reduction in the capital-labor ratio, interindustry shifts of workers, intersectoral shifts of capital and a reduction in the overall experience of the labor force as more young workers entered it.[4] However, they were unable to explain a slowdown in the productivity growth rate between 1965 and 1973.

The failure of these fairly orthodox explanations to account fully for the productivity slowdown has stimulated the development of non-classical models which attempt to breach the gap. Weisskopf, Bowles and Gordon argued that the decline in productivity growth stems from declining work intensity and lagging business innovation due to more friction in the workplace and a reduction in the frequency of business failures.[5] Richard Nelson, in his survey of research on productivity growth, mentioned several studies focussing on such issues as workplace organization, marketplace pressures on the firm, and workers' lives outside their jobs.[6] Jeffrey Sachs, using current and lagged unemployment rates to explain labor productivity growth in manufacturing, found that although a high unemployment rate reduces productivity growth in the short run due to the well-known procyclicality of productivity, it will ultimately boost productivity growth. He argued that a reduction in profits (which is correlated with increases in the unemployment rate) boosts productivity if it drives inefficient firms out of business. Sachs also speculated that firms face less opposition from unions and workers toward reducing employment when profits are low. In the short run, however, the firm is expected to hoard labor.[7]

Several of these nontraditional explanations for the productivity slowdown imply an interaction between profits and productivity growth—low profits put pressure on the firm to become more efficient, reducing labor costs and thus boosting measured productivity. Indeed, the idea that high profits reduce productivity growth goes back at least to Adam Smith:

The high rate of profit seems every where to destroy that parsimony which in other circumstances is natural to the character of the merchant. When profits are high, that sober virtue seems to be superfluous, and expensive luxury to suit better the affluence of his situation.[8]

In this chapter, I seek to both document the relationship between profits and productivity somewhat more carefully than past researchers, taking into account the procyclical nature of both profits and productivity, and flesh out some theories relating profits to productivity, providing empirical tests where possible. The results, although sometimes not statistically significant, indicate that, even when the cyclical component of profits is removed and other possible explanations of a negative profits-productivity correlation are accounted for, low profits stimulate productivity growth.

Chart 1.2 provides some visual evidence for the claim that high profits affect productivity adversely, at least since 1970. The chart shows a three-year moving average of nonfinancial after-tax corporate profits, as a percentage of nonfinancial corporate GDP (both excluding petroleum refining), plotted with a three-year moving average of cyclically-adjusted labor productivity growth for the nonfinancial corporate sector. Slow productivity growth in the 1970s coincided with a high profit share, while more rapid productivity growth in the 1980s occured during a period of low profits. Productivity growth decelerated at the end of the 1980s while profitability was improving.

The second section of this chapter presents a simple model of labor productivity growth and documents the basic empirical result of this study: using quarterly data, the first two lags of the profit share have a significant adverse impact on labor productivity growth, controlling for the normal cyclical behavior of productivity. Further tests indicate that part of the effect of high or low profits is temporary, but more than half of the effect is permanent. The basic finding—an almost significant adverse effect of profits on labor productivity growth—is repeated using annual data.

The third section tests whether the apparent econometric link between profits and productivity growth is robust with respect to alternative explanations. In particular, several hypotheses based on the premise that the profits-productivity relationship results from inadequately controlling for the business cycle are proposed and tested. The only test which reduces the estimated coefficient of profits

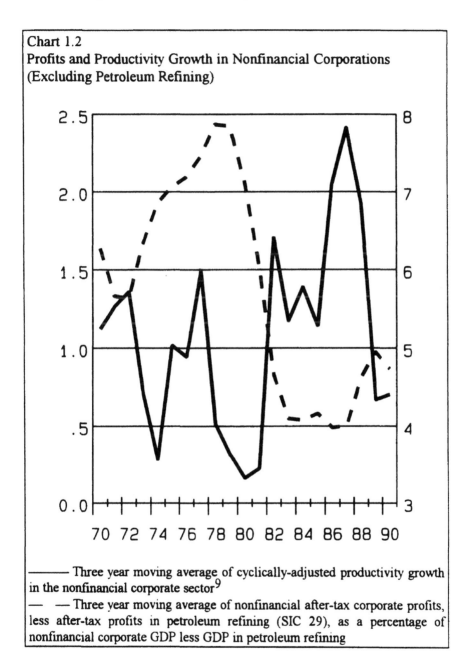

Chart 1.2
Profits and Productivity Growth in Nonfinancial Corporations
(Excluding Petroleum Refining)

————— Three year moving average of cyclically-adjusted productivity growth in the nonfinancial corporate sector[9]
— — Three year moving average of nonfinancial after-tax corporate profits, less after-tax profits in petroleum refining (SIC 29), as a percentage of nonfinancial corporate GDP less GDP in petroleum refining

significantly is the addition of lagged values of the ratio of actual to potential GNP. These ratios themselves, however, are not significant, indicating multicollinearity with the profit share.

Section 4 separates profits into cyclical (i.e., temporary) and noncyclical (i.e., permanent) components for both U.S. manufacturing industries and for the aggregate manufacturing sectors of four other OECD countries. Although the cyclical component of profits is generally found to have a larger negative effect on labor productivity growth, noncyclical profits have a more statistically significant effect. Among other OECD countries, the sign on the noncyclical profits coefficient is correct in three of the four cases tested, but significant only in West Germany.

Section 5 surveys the only relevant literature on the profits-productivity relationship that I am aware of—the "satisficing" literature. The general idea of these papers is that when profits fall below some threshold level, a firm takes steps to restore profitability, at least partially by cutting costs. Low profits can be said to cause higher productivity when such cuts in costs mean a reduction in the amount of labor needed to produce a given amount of output. Although I do not think the satisficing literature is adequate—the version found in most papers can only explain temporary increases in productivity, which are outweighed in my empirical results by permanent increases—it provides a convenient reference point for the theories this chapter proposes as well as some useful case study evidence.

Section 6 presents one possible explanation for the profits-productivity nexus: a model in which managers allocate time between cost-cutting activities and sales-increasing activities. High profits per unit of sales (a high profit share) increase the returns from activities which increase sales, and thus cause managers to spend less time controlling costs. In addition, when profits per unit of sales are high, firms may replace managers who are good at containing costs with those who are adept at increasing sales, having the same effect. When profits per sale are low, managers shift their attention to cutting costs, and some managers less adept at cutting costs may be replaced. In such a world, the answer to whether or not a productivity slowdown resulting from high profits is bad for general welfare depends on whether the activities which increase sales generate positive effects, e.g., new innovations or better service, or simply shift demand from one firm to another, e.g., advertising.

An alternative explanation for why low profits stimulate productivity growth is that, when faced with the prospect of losing their jobs through the bankruptcy of their company or a shutdown of their plant, groups within the firm will be willing to adopt more efficient practices. Section 7 presents a simple liquidity constraint hypothesis, in which workers lose their jobs when their employer becomes insolvent, and reviews some empirical evidence relating to this hypothesis.

Section 8 outlines a second version of the bankruptcy hypothesis, which has different testable implications from the liquidity constraint version. In the "bankruptcy by choice" model, the firm declares bankruptcy not necessarily when profits are negative, but when the present discounted value from use of the assets of the firm is less than the value of the assets if sold. (In the case of an individual plant, the firm must also take account of the effect of the plant's production on the prices received for products made at the firm's other plants.) Because such a decision will be made on the basis of profits over a long time horizon, noncyclical (permanent) profits will be more important than cyclical (transitory) profits. In contrast, the liquidity constraint model focuses on the short run, so expected profits over a fairly short time horizon will be all that matters, whether such profits are cyclical or not. As noted above, the evidence indicates that noncyclical profits have a more statistically significant impact on productivity growth.

Section 9 takes disaggregation a step further, presenting the results obtained by regressions for the Big Three auto makers. These firms provide strong support for the bankruptcy by choice hypothesis —labor productivity growth responds positively to low noncyclical profits but not to profits which are low due to weak demand. Section 10 summarizes and concludes.

2. BASIC EMPIRICAL FINDINGS

This section of the chapter sets out a simple model of labor productivity growth, modified to account for the effects of profits on productivity. Profits can affect productivity either temporarily or permanently. The temporary effect is captured by a transitory change in the parameter governing effort. High profits can have a permanent effect on productivity growth if they somehow cause changes in the technology of production. Such changes include more efficient organization of work, i.e., the use of fewer workers to accomplish the same task. Estimating a labor hours equation using quarterly data, we find both of the effects to be present, but the latter dominates.

Model

Following the analyses of Sims and Clark,[10] labor costs exclusive of the wage consist of adjustment and "disequilibrium" costs. These are given by

$$(1.1) \qquad C_t = 0.5b(L_t - L_{t-1})^2 + 0.5c(L_t - L*_t)^2,$$

where L is the logarithm of total hours of labor and L* is the logarithm of the stock of "effective" hours, upon which production itself actually depends. The first term represents the cost of adjusting labor hours over time, which may be due either to adjusting the stock of workers (costs of hiring and firing) or to adjusting hours per worker (for example, overtime costs).

The second term is added because any model of short run labor demand must explain the paradox of short run increasing returns to labor, or "SRIRL".[11] That is, over the short run, a given percentage change in output is accomplished with less than equal percentage changes in labor hours and fixed capital. L* is normally interpreted as the amount of labor hours needed assuming no SRIRL, and is thus roughly proportional to output. In the short run, the firm can respond to an increase in output (and thus in L*) by boosting L less than L*. The second term of equation (1.1) is the cost to the firm of doing this.

The literature is not clear as to what this cost is. Sims and Clark refer to L* as "desired" hours, but fail to give a reason why the firm should desire that level of hours. I argue that effective hours in excess of actual hours is accounted for in the production function by another input, "effort." The cost of L* being above L is thus the cost of "effort." Unfortunately, equation (1.1) implies not only that costs increase as effort is increased above "normal" (defined as L=L*) but that costs increase as effort is *decreased* below normal. Since it is difficult to think of costs related to effort which would not increase monotonically with effort, equation (1.1) rests on shaky theoretical ground.

Most studies of productivity use a quadratic cost specification such as that of equation (1.1) because, after minimization, actual labor hours depend linearly on L*, which in turn is assumed to be a linear function of output. In revising the equation to more properly account for effort, this helpful property is retained. (A more detailed treatment of effort is discussed in the second chapter of this book.)

In the labor hours model of this section, equation (1.1) is replaced by

$$(1.2) \quad C_t = 0.5b(L_t - L_{t-1})^2 + 0.5c(X_t + L*_t - L_t)^2 + cL_tX'.$$

X_t measures the difficulty of obtaining effort from workers, and is normalized to be always positive so that a reduction in L below L* reduces, rather than increases, effort costs. X' is defined as the steady state level of X_t. The final term assures that the firm's steady state $(L_t = L_{t-1}, X_t = X')$ optimal solution is to set $L_t = L*_t$.

According to equation (1.2), a drop in X_t means that any given level of effort can be obtained more cheaply. Thus, one way that low profits can raise productivity is by reducing X, thus reducing the amount of L (actual hours) for a given amount of L* (production).

The firm desires to minimize the present discounted value of future costs, $E_t \Sigma R^s C_{t+s}$, where R is the discount rate and E_t denotes expectations at time t. We assume that R is constant over time. Solving the first order conditions for L_t, we find

$$(1.3) \quad L_t = \frac{b}{b+bR+c}L_{t-1} + \frac{bR}{b+bR+c}E_tL_{t+1} + \frac{c}{b+bR+c}L*_t$$
$$+ \frac{c}{b+bR+c}X_t - \frac{c}{b+bR+c}X'.$$

This can be rewritten (see Appendix A) as

$$(1.4) \quad L_t = \beta_1 L_{t-1} + (1-\beta_1)L*_t + \beta_3(X_t - X')$$
$$+ (1-\beta_1)(1-\beta_2)\sum_{i=1}^{\infty}\beta_2{}^i(E_tL*_{t+i} - L*_t),$$

where $(1-\beta_1) \geq \beta_3 \geq (1-\beta_1)(1-\beta_2)$. β_3 depends on the expected persistence of deviations in X_t from X'. If deviations are temporary, $\beta_3 = (1-\beta_1)(1-\beta_2)$, while if deviations are permanent, $\beta_3 = 1-\beta_1$. Actual labor hours thus depend on lagged hours, effective hours, expected hours, and the relative difficulty of extracting extra effort from workers. In standard labor demand models, the effort term is absent, so equation (1.4) becomes

$$L_t = \beta_1 L_{t-1} + (1-\beta_1)L*_t$$

(1.5)
$$+ (1-\beta_1)(1-\beta_2)\sum_{i=1}^{\infty}\beta_2^{i}(E_t L*_{t+i} - L*_t).$$

L* and K*, effective labor and capital, are the true inputs in production. I assume that production takes place according to a standard Cobb-Douglas production function, which in logarithms is

(1.6) $Y_t = A_t + aL*_t + (1-a)K*_t,$

where Y is the logarithm of real output and A is a parameter reflecting productivity. This expression can be rewritten as

(1.7) $L*_t = Y_t - A_t + (1-a)(L*_t - K*_t).$

The literature on short run labor productivity growth generally assumes that $(L*_t - K*_t)$ can be captured by a constant trend.[12] I also will make the same assumption here.

A_t, the state of technology, depends on both the rate of new innovation and improvements in the factor inputs themselves. While the latter are probably well described by some trend terms, the former may contain quite a bit of movement from quarter to quarter. Thus, the assumption that labor productivity is a simple upward time trend is incorrect. Ignoring for the moment the profit effect which this chapter discusses, I assume the rate of innovation is white noise around a trend, so that $\Delta A_t = z + e_t$. We then have

(1.8) $A_t = A_0 + zt + \sum_{i=0}^{N-1}e_{t-i},$

where $A_{t-N} = A_0$. Substituting this into equation (1.7) produces

(1.9) $L*_t = Y_t - A_0 - z't - \sum_{i=0}^{N-1}e_{t-i},$

where $z' = z - (1-a)$(trend rate of growth in L*–K*).

Given this expression for the logarithm of effective labor hours, two different specifications for the change in labor hours can be derived. I will show that the first—a standard specification which is commonly used in the literature—has a moving average error term. I then derive the specification used in this chapter, which has a white noise error term.

To simplify the derivation of the standard specification, assume static expectations (as did Fair),[13] i.e., $E_t L^*_{t+i} = L^*_t$. Equation (1.5) simplifies to

(1.10) $\quad L_t = \beta_1 L_{t-1} + (1 - \beta_1) L^*_t$.

Substituting for L^*_t from equation (1.9), we have

$$L_t = \beta_1 L_{t-1} + (1 - \beta_1) Y_t - (1 - \beta_1) z't - (1 - \beta_1) A_0$$
(1.11)
$$- (1 - \beta_1) \sum_{i=0}^{\infty} e_{t-i} .$$

Subtracting L_{t-1} from both sides, we get

$$\Delta L_t = (1 - \beta_1)(Y_t - L_{t-1}) - (1 - \beta_1) z't - (1 - \beta_1) A_0$$
(1.12)
$$- (1 - \beta_1) \sum_{i=0}^{\infty} e_{t-i} .$$

Given that the error term is a moving average, it is no surprise that Clark found very strong serial correlation in the errors ($\rho = 0.65$) when he estimated this equation.[14] To eliminate the moving average error term, we must use a different expression for the change in labor hours.[15]

Before discussing such an alternative specification, we must address the issue of expected changes in labor hours, which are contained in equation (1.4), the starting point for this alternative specification. The literature generally assumes that expected future increases in effective labor hours, i.e., expected future increases in output less the trend in productivity, are equal to zero. In this chapter, however, such an assumption is problematic because one can argue that the level of profits is correlated with expected future changes in output. A firm which expects higher future output will begin to increase labor hours now in order to reduce future adjustment costs. For this reason, profits and labor productivity could display a spurious negative correlation.

By rearranging the final term, equation (1.4) can be rewritten as

$$L_t = \beta_1 L_{t-1} + (1-\beta_1)L*_t + \beta_3(X_t - X')$$

(1.13) $$+ (1-\beta_1)\beta_2(E_t L*_{t+1} - L*_t)$$

$$+ (1-\beta_1)(1-\beta_2)\sum_{i=2}^{\infty}\beta_2^i (E_t L*_{t+i} - E_t L*_{t+1}).$$

The firm should have a reasonably good idea of how its labor needs will change between the current and succeeding quarter. For more distant periods, however, as well as on an annual basis, this is unlikely. In such periods, we assume expected growth in the logarithm of effective hours equals C, a constant. Hence, $E_t L*_{t+i} - E_t L*_{t+1}$ equals $(i-1)C$.

Substituting for the L* terms using equation (1.9) and taking first differences, equation (1.13) becomes

$$\Delta L_t = \beta_1 \Delta L_{t-1} + (1-\beta_1)\Delta Y_t + \beta_3 \Delta X_t + (1-\beta_1)\beta_2 E_t \Delta Y_{t+1}$$

(1.14) $$+ \frac{(1-\beta_1)\beta_2^2}{1-\beta_2} C - (1-\beta_1)z' - (1-\beta_1)e_t.$$

Profits can enter equation (1.14) in two ways: through X, the difficulty of obtaining effort from workers, which is reduced when profits are low; or through a change in the technology of production, captured by e, the non-time trend component of labor productivity growth.

The theoretical models in sections 6, 7 and 8 of this chapter indicate that profits affect productivity with a lag—profits either signal a firm's dire financial straits to its workers or cause the firm to redirect managerial effort towards cutting costs from increasing sales. Productivity will thus not respond to current or expected future profits. Past profits may be important, however, since there is no reason to assume that the effects set in motion by high or low profits die out after just one period. The change in X will thus be some function of past changes in profits:

(1.15)
$$\Delta X_t = \mu_1(AQ_{t-1} - AQ_{t-2}) + \mu_2(AQ_{t-2} - AQ_{t-3}) + \ldots$$
$$= \mu_1 AQ_{t-1} + (\mu_2 - \mu_1)AQ_{t-2} + (\mu_3 - \mu_2)AQ_{t-3} + \ldots,$$

where AQ is the profit share (defined below). Similarly, changes in the technology of production may not follow immediately after a change in profits, so that

(1.16) $$e_t = \gamma_1 AQ_{t-1} + \gamma_2 AQ_{t-2} + \ldots + u_t,$$

where u is a white noise error uncorrelated with the right hand side variables of equation (1.14).

Substituting equations (1.15) and (1.16) into equation (1.14) produces

$$
\begin{aligned}
\Delta L_t = {} & (1-\beta_1)\beta_2^{\,2}(1-\beta_2)C - (1-\beta_1)z' \\
& + \beta_1 \Delta L_{t-1} + (1-\beta_1)\Delta Y_t + (1-\beta_1)\beta_2 E_t \Delta Y_{t+1} \\
& + \left[\gamma_1(1-\beta_1) + \beta_3\mu_1\right]AQ_{t-1} \\
& + \left[\gamma_2(1-\beta_1) + \beta_3(\mu_2-\mu_1)\right]AQ_{t-2} \\
& + \left[\gamma_3(1-\beta_1) + \beta_3(\mu_3-\mu_2)\right]AQ_{t-3} + \ldots + u_t
\end{aligned}
$$

(1.17)

With no way to identify the μ and γ, equation (1.17) must be estimated in reduced form. However, the sum of the coefficients on the AQ in equation (1.15) are zero (only a *change* in profits increases effort). Thus, the sum of the coefficients on the AQ in equation (1.17) will be positive only if the profits-productivity relationship is at least partially caused by permanent changes in the technology of production (changes in e). To the extent that some of the higher lags of AQ have negative coefficients, we have proof that profits affect productivity growth via changes in effort (changes in X).

Data: Quarterly

Profits are defined as net income after taxes for manufacturing except petroleum refining, from the Bureau of the Census' Quarterly Financial Report program, seasonally adjusted using the X-11-ARIMA method. The profit share variable, AQ, equals this measure of profits divided by national income for manufacturing, without capital consumption adjustment, also seasonally adjusted. Profits for petroleum and coal products (SIC 29) are excluded both because their share in manufacturing profits is much larger than their share in manufacturing value added, and because profits for petroleum refining are correlated with high oil prices, which may exert their own negative influence on manufacturing productivity growth.

In the regressions using quarterly data, labor hours are the BLS index of total hours paid for all manufacturing workers (1977=1.0), seasonally adjusted. The output measure used is the BLS output index for the manufacturing sector (1977=1.0). Estimates of $E_t\Delta Y_{t+1}$ are obtained as the fitted values from an eighth order vector autoregression on ΔY_t, ΔL_t, and the profit share.

Results: Quarterly Data

The equation

$$
(1.18) \quad
\begin{aligned}
\Delta L_t = {} & c_0 + c_1 \Delta Y_t + c_2 \Delta L_{t-1} + c_3 E_t \Delta Y_{t+1} \\
& + d_1 A Q_{t-1} + \ldots + d_N A Q_{t-N},
\end{aligned}
$$

where Δ denotes percent change, was estimated for the sample period 1952:4 to 1988:2. The choice of how many lags of profits to use is a difficult one. Pagano and Hartley suggested starting with a large number of lags, and removing lags until one can no longer reject the joint hypothesis that the coefficients of the removed lags all equal zero.[16] This hypothesis, however, can already be rejected at the 99% level for the eighth lag. The second and third columns of Table 1.1 show the results obtained from estimating equation (1.18) with two different polynomial distributed lag specifications for profits, each with eight lags.

The sum of coefficients on the change in output, the lagged change in hours and the expected change in output is close to unity, as predicted by the theory. More importantly, using either a third- or fourth-degree PDL, the sum of the coefficients on the lagged profit share terms is significantly positive at the 99.5% level. As shown in the discussion above, this means that a temporary deviation in profits from its normal level will cause a permanent change in the level of labor hours.

The results also provide some evidence that deviations in profits have an additional temporary effect on productivity—the coefficients of the first three lags of profits using the 4th order PDL sum to 299.4, while the sum of all coefficients is only 187.8. The difference, 111.6, compares with a standard error of 55.1 for the sum of the eight coefficients. Testing the hypothesis that profits have a temporary effect with a 3rd order PDL, however, we find that the sum of the coefficients on the first two lags (the third is negative) is just 195.8, while the sum of all eight coefficients is 177.4. The difference, 17.6, is not significant. Thus, while a permanent impact of profit share on productivity is strongly significant, the data offer no firm conclusion as to whether changes in the level of profits cause temporary changes in labor productivity—in the model above, changes in effort—as well.

Table 1.1
Effect of Profits on Labor Demand

		Fourth degree PDL of AQ	Third degree PDL of AQ	Two lags of AQ
Constant	-1.71**	-7.60**	-7.17**	-6.13**
	(0.23)	(1.70)	(1.74)	(1.45)
%ch(JQM)	0.51**	0.46**	0.49**	0.51**
	(0.03)	(0.04)	(0.04)	(0.03)
%ch(JMHM\1)	0.30**	0.27**	0.25**	0.29**
	(0.03)	(0.04)	(0.04)	(0.04)
EY	0.11*	0.24**	0.18**	0.17**
	(0.05)	(0.06)	(0.05)	(0.05)
AQ\1		25.7	158.9*	21.7
		(89.2)	(79.9)	(94.2)
AQ\2		229.1**	37.0	121.7
		(69.4)	(28.4)	(94.4)
AQ\3		44.6	-19.0	
		(49.3)	(46.0)	
AQ\4		-134.0**	-29.0	
		(47.3)	(32.8)	
AQ\5		-119.0**	-11.5	
		(44.3)	(27.1)	
AQ\6		70.3*	12.7	
		(43.9)	(40.7)	
AQ\7		208.4**	24.3	
		(67.0)	(28.6)	
AQ\8		-137.3*	3.6	
		(77.6)	(63.9)	
Sum of		187.8**	177.4**	143.4**
lagged AQ		(55.1)	(56.7)	(46.6)

Notes: The dependent variable is %ch(JMHM), the annual rate of change in the index of manufacturing hours. %ch(JQM) is the annual rate of change in real manufacturing output. %ch(JMHM\1) is %ch(JMHM) lagged one quarter. EY is the forecasted rate of change in real manufacturing output for the following quarter. AQ\i is the profit share described in the text, lagged i quarters. * denotes significance at the 95% level. ** denotes significance at the 99% level. All regressions were estimated using quarterly data for 1952:4 to 1988:2. Figures in parentheses are standard errors.

Given the weakness of the temporary change result relative to the permanent change result, the rest of the chapter focuses on permanent changes in productivity. Since we thus turn our attention toward the sum of the profits coefficients, rather than their distribution, a specification using fewer lags is preferred. Amemiya suggested that for quarterly data, two or three lags are generally optimal.[17] Since the first two lags of profits have positive coefficients in both the PDLs tested,

Table 1.2
Effect of Profits and Time Dummies on Labor Demand

Constant	-1.71**	-7.83**
	(0.35)	(1.64)
%ch(JQM)	0.52**	0.50**
	(0.03)	(0.03)
%ch(JMHM\1)	0.30**	0.27**
	(0.03)	(0.04)
EY	0.11*	0.18*
	(0.05)	(0.05)
DUMMY1	-0.06	-0.73
	(0.55)	(0.56)
DUMMY2	0.09	-0.45
	(0.55)	(0.54)
AQ\1		75.0
		(96.3)
AQ\2		144.9
		(94.0)
Sum of		219.9**
lagged AQ		(57.7)

Notes: The dependent variable is %ch(JMHM), the annual rate of change in the index of manufacturing hours. %ch(JQM) is the annual rate of change in real manufacturing output. %ch(JMHM\1) is %ch(JMHM) lagged one quarter. EY is the forecasted rate of change in real manufacturing output for the following quarter. DUMMY1 is zero from 1952:4 to 1966:3 and unity from 1966:4 to 1988:2. DUMMY2 is zero from 1952:4 to 1973:3 and unity from 1973:4 to 1988:2. AQ\i is the profit share described in the text, lagged i quarters. * denotes significance at the 95% level. ** denotes significance at the 99% level. All regressions were estimated using quarterly data for 1952:4 to 1988:2. Figures in parentheses are standard errors.

and because the third lag can be rejected using the Pagano-Hartley criterion, regressions using quarterly data are run with two lags of profits for the rest of the chapter.

The results of estimating equation (1.18) with two lags of the profit share are shown in the final column of Table 1.1. The sum of coefficients on the change in output, the expected change in output and the lagged change in labor hours sum to 0.95, which is very close to the value of unity predicted by the theory. The sum of the profits coefficients is significantly positive at the 99% level.

Any regression of labor hours should take account of possible changes in the trend rate of change of productivity growth, z. Productivity slowdowns are widely acknowledged to have occurred in 1966 and 1973 (e.g., by Denison).[18] A dummy taking the value one for

1966:4 and all subsequent quarters (DUMMY1) and a dummy taking the value one for 1973:4 and all subsequent quarters (DUMMY2) are added to equation (1.18). Without the profits variables in the equation, the 1973 slowdown dummy has a positive, although insignificant, coefficient (Table 1.2), supporting the existence of a productivity slowdown. Once profits are added, however, an independent role for the slowdown dummies disappears, meaning profits hold some potential for explaining the productivity slowdown. In neither case (with or without profits) is there evidence for a slowdown of labor productivity in the 1960s, which agrees with Griliches' finding for manufacturing.[19]

Equation (1.18) contains the potential for simultaneity. From at least the early 1970s,[20] studies of cyclical productivity have recognized that if higher productivity (i.e., lower unit labor requirements) leads to higher output, the coefficient of output will be biased downward. In general, however, this same literature does not instrument for output. Equation (1.18) was run using the change in real GNP (in 1982 dollars) as an instrument for the change in manufacturing output. The coeffecient on output becomes larger, as the above discussion suggests. However, the coefficient on expected output becomes slightly negative, and the sum of coefficients on current output, lagged labor hours and expected output drops to 0.84. Even with the inclusion of the profit share, the coefficient on expected output remains tiny, so it is excluded from the regressions whenever instruments are used for the change in output. Table 1.3 shows the results with and without the lagged profit share. Although the sum of profit share coefficients is reduced slightly by instrumenting for output, it remains significant at the 99% level.

Given the close relationship between GNP and manufacturing output, the former may be an inadequate instrument for the latter. As an alternative, the current change in real money and its first lag were used as instruments. Money is defined here as M1—the sum of currency and checkable deposits. The results are very similar to those using GNP as an instrument, except that the standard errors are much higher. The sum of the profits coefficients is only significant at the 97.5% level, although it is slightly larger than that obtained using real GNP as an instrument.

Less macro-oriented studies of labor demand generally include some measure of labor cost. To see what effects this might have, a second-order PDL of the contemporaneous change in real compensation and its first three lags was added to equation (1.18).

Table 1.3
Effect of Profits on Labor Demand, Using Instrumental Variables

	Instrument for %ch(JQM)		
	Real GNP	Real GNP	Current and Lagged Real Money
Constant	-1.66**	-5.54**	-5.51**
	(0.22)	(1.48)	(1.91)
%ch(JQM)	0.62**	0.64**	0.64**
	(0.03)	(0.03)	(0.07)
%ch(JMHM\1)	0.24**	0.22**	0.22**
	(0.03)	(0.04)	(0.05)
AQ\1		25.1	25.6
		(99.0)	(101.5)
AQ\2		103.2	101.9
		(98.3)	(113.5)
Sum of		128.3**	127.5*
lagged AQ		(48.0)	(58.8)

Notes: The dependent variable is %ch(JMHM), the annual rate of change in the index of manufacturing hours. %ch(JQM) is the annual rate of change in real manufacturing output. %ch(JMHM\1) is %ch(JMHM) lagged one quarter. AQ\i is the profit share described in the text, lagged i quarters. * denotes significance at the 95% level. ** denotes significance at the 99% level. All regressions were estimated using quarterly data for 1952:4 to 1988:2. Figures in parentheses are standard errors.

Real compensation is defined here as compensation per hour in manufacturing divided by the implicit price deflator for GNP (1982=100). We expect the coefficients on the real wage and its lags to sum to the negative of labor's share of total compensation. The sum of coefficients, however, is never larger than 0.32 in absolute value in an equation without profits or 0.22 in an equation including profits (Table 1.4). Most importantly, the sum of the profits coefficients is virtually unchanged.

Data: Annual

The tests were also performed using annual data. One advantage of going to an annual frequency is that output data are available on a two-digit industry basis, allowing tests at a more disaggregated level. As we shall see in later sections, variations in the characteristics of these industries enable us to test hypotheses concerning the source of the profits-productivity relationship.

Table 1.4
Effect of Profits and Real Compensation on Labor Demand

Constant	-1.20**	-4.52**
	(0.33)	(1.68)
%ch(JQM)	0.62**	0.64**
	(0.03)	(0.03)
%ch(JMHM\1)	0.23**	0.22**
	(0.03)	(0.04)
%ch(W)	-0.07	-0.07
	(0.09)	(0.09)
%ch(W\1)	-0.01	-0.00
	(0.06)	(0.06)
%ch(W\2)	-0.05	-0.02
	(0.06)	(0.07)
%ch(W\3)	-0.18*	-0.13
	(0.08)	(0.09)
Sum of	-0.32*	-0.22
%ch(W\i)	(0.16)	(0.18)
AQ\1		-6.6
		(102.2)
AQ\2		111.4
		(99.6)
Sum of		104.8*
lagged AQ		(51.3)

Notes: The dependent variable is %ch(JMHM), the annual rate of change in the index of manufacturing hours. %ch(JQM) is the annual rate of change in real manufacturing output. %ch(JMHM\1) is %ch(JMHM) lagged one quarter. %ch(W\i) is the ith lag of the percentage change in real compensation in manufacturing. AQ\i is the profit share described in the text, lagged i quarters. Real GNP growth was used as an instrument for %ch(JQM). * denotes significance at the 95% level. ** denotes significance at the 99% level. Both regressions were estimated using quarterly data for 1952:4 to 1988:2. Figures in parentheses are standard errors.

To maintain consistency with data available at the industry level and to test the robustness of the profits-productivity result with respect to variations in the specification of productivity, I redefine output and hours worked. Output is defined as real GDP (in 1982 dollars) in manufacturing, while hours are manufacturing employment times average weekly hours of manufacturing production workers. Once again, real GNP is used as an instrument. The forecasted change in future output had the wrong sign, so it was excluded from the regressions.

In tests performed at the two-digit SIC code level, the variables used were defined the same way as in the aggregate manufacturing

Table 1.5
Effect of Profits on Labor Demand: Annual Data

Constant	-2.11**	-4.73**
	(0.30)	(1.80)
%ch(GDP82)	0.82**	0.82**
	(0.04)	(0.04)
%ch(LM\1)	0.11*	0.08
	(0.05)	(0.05)
AQ\1		25.2
		(16.9)

Notes: The dependent variable, %ch(LM), is the percent growth in worker hours in manufacturing. %ch(GDP82) is the percentage change in real manufacturing GDP. %ch(LM\1) is %ch(LM), lagged one quarter. AQ\1 is the first lag of the profit share variable described in the text. Real GNP growth was used as an instrument for %ch(GDP82). * denotes significance at the 95% level. ** denotes significance at the 99% level. Both regressions were estimated using annual data for 1950 to 1987. Figures in parentheses are standard errors.

case. The change in real GNP was used as an instrument for the change in output in each of the regressions.

Results: Annual

For aggregate manufacturing (Table 1.5), the coefficients on the change in output and the lagged change in labor hours sum to less than unity, as in the case of quarterly data using instruments. The coefficient on the lagged profit share, unfortunately, is significant only at the 90% level. The reduction in significance, however, is due more to an increase in the standard error than to a reduction in the coefficient—the coefficient on the lagged profit share falls to 25.2 using annual data, compared to a sum of 32.1 using quarterly data and instruments, while the standard error jumps to 16.9 from 12.0. (The figure 32.1 is found by dividing 128.3, the actual quarterly result, by 4. We must do this because the dependent variable in the quarterly regressions is an annual, rather than a quarterly, rate of change.)

In fact, redefining labor hours as the Census Bureau's hours of full-time and part-time workers, we find that the coefficient on lagged profits rises to 28.3, significant at the 95% level. Unfortunately, this series was discontinued for 2-digit industries in 1978. To provide more degrees of freedom, industry regressions were performed using the product of hours and employees. Because the results for aggregate

Table 1.6
Effect of Profits on Labor Demand, by Industry

	Textiles (22)	Paper (26)	Chemicals (28)	Petroleum (29)
Constant	-15.2*	-4.1*	-16.7**	-10.1*
	(7.1)	(2.3)	(6.2)	(5.1)
%ch(GDP82)	1.09**	0.60**	0.84**	1.02
	(0.27)	(0.10)	(0.25)	(0.64)
%ch(L\1)	-0.39*	0.28*	0.84**	0.15
	(0.24)	(0.15)	(0.25)	(0.28)
AQ\1	133.6	22.2	59.5*	8.3*
	(85.4)	(19.1)	(26.2)	(4.3)

	Stone, Clay and Glass (32)	Primary Metals (33)	Fabricated Metals (34)	Nonelectrical Machinery (35)
Constant	-2.92	-1.66*	-4.2**	-5.2
	(1.81)	(0.87)	(1.6)	(4.2)
%ch(GDP82)	0.83**	0.72**	0.95**	0.95**
	(0.07)	(0.05)	(0.05)	(0.12)
%ch(L\1)	0.21**	-0.06	0.11*	0.10
	(0.08)	(0.06)	(0.05)	(0.11)
AQ\1	10.8	7.2	31.4	15.1
	(16.6)	(7.0)	(21.3)	(35.0)

	Electrical Machinery (36)	Motor Vehicles (371)	Other Transportation (372@9)
Constant	-4.1	-0.9	-8.5*
	(3.9)	(2.3)	(3.7)
%ch(GDP82)	0.84**	0.70**	1.21**
	(0.09)	(0.06)	(0.16)
%ch(L\1)	-0.02	0.15	-0.26*
	(0.08)	(0.09)	(0.13)
AQ\1	9.6	-11.1	93.7*
	(35.8)	(16.4)	(49.5)

Notes: The dependent variable in each case, %ch(L), is the percentage change in the industry's labor hours. %ch(GDP82) is the percent change in each industry's real GDP. %ch(L\1) is %ch(L), lagged one year. AQ\1 is the lag of the profit share described in the text. In each case, the percentage change in real GNP is used to instrument for %ch(GDP82). * denotes significance at the 95% level. ** denotes significance at the 99% level. All regressions were estimated using annual data for 1950 to 1987. Figures in parentheses are either industry SIC codes or standard errors, where applicable.

manufacturing are weaker than those obtained using hours of full-time and part-time workers, the results for the two-digit industries are also probably weaker than if the full-time and part-time hours data were available for the full sample period.

Regressions were performed on two-digit SIC codes for which the profits measure was available. Those were textiles (22), paper (26), chemicals (28), petroleum and coal products (29), stone, clay and glass (32), primary metals (33), fabricated metals (34), nonelectrical machinery (35), and electrical machinery (36). The data allow us to split transportation equipment (37) into motor vehicles and parts (371) and other transportation equipment (372@9). Although the coefficient on lagged profits is positive for ten of the eleven industries (Table 1.6), it is significantly positive for only three—chemicals, petroleum refining and other transportation equipment.

3. HOW ROBUST ARE THE BASIC RESULTS?

Before considering possible sources of the profits-productivity relationship in sections 4 through 8, this section examines whether profits are simply proxying for some other variable which has been omitted from the labor hours regressions. In general, although some of the tested variables succeed in reducing the significance of lagged profits, none reduces the sum of coefficients by as much as 50%. Thus, although we can weaken the basic result, we cannot get rid of it.

The most common criticism directed at the basic result of this chapter—that low profits stimulate productivity growth—has been that the full complexity of the business cycle is not captured in the simple labor productivity model of Section 2, and that the positive coefficient on lagged profits thus captures the effects of some important excluded variable. Consequently, three sets of variables are added to the labor hours equation to correct for this potential problem—a polynomial distributed lag of the ratio of actual to potential GNP, Robert Gordon's "end-of-expansion" variable, and William Dickens' modification of Gordon's test. In the latter two cases, we will show that even though the added variables are significant, the significance of the profits effect is virtually unchanged. In the case of the ratio of actual to potential GNP, the results are somewhat more ambiguous.

Table 1.7

Effect of Profits on Labor Demand, Controlling for Ratios of Actual to Potential GNP

Constant	-19.0**	-17.0**	-14.6*	-12.4*
	(5.8)	(6.0)	(6.0)	(6.2)
%ch(JQM)	0.50**	0.50**	0.64**	0.65**
	(0.03)	(0.03)	(0.03)	(0.03)
%ch(JMHM\1)	0.29**	0.28**	0.21**	0.20**
	(0.05)	(0.06)	(0.05)	(0.06)
EY	0.20**	0.21**		
	(0.06)	(0.06)		
GNPRATIO\1	-2.3	-2.8	0.7	0.2
	(32.4)	(32.6)	(34.5)	(35.0)
GNPRATIO\2	22.8	15.8	12.9	6.3
	(29.3)	(30.1)	(30.9)	(32.1)
GNPRATIO\3	22.0	20.4	17.7	15.9
	(17.3)	(17.4)	(18.4)	(18.6)
GNPRATIO\4	2.8	7.3	7.5	11.3
	(25.9)	(26.3)	(27.6)	(28.3)
GNPRATIO\5	-27.3	-27.3	-25.2	-24.9
	(20.9)	(20.8)	(22.2)	(22.3)
Sum of lagged	18.0**	13.3*	13.6*	8.9
GNPRATIO	(6.1)	(6.9)	(6.3)	(7.2)
AQ\1		21.7		30.3
		(95.2)		(101.9)
AQ\2		59.6		45.2
		(97.8)		(104.7)
Sum of		81.3		75.5
lagged AQ		(52.7)		(56.6)
Instrument for %ch(JQM)	no	no	yes	yes

Notes: The dependent variable is %ch(JMHM), the annual rate of change in the index of manufacturing hours. %ch(JQM) is the annual rate of change in real manufacturing output. %ch(JMHM\1) is %ch(JMHM) lagged one quarter. EY is the forecasted rate of change in real manufacturing output for the following quarter. GNPRATIO\i is the ith lag of the ratio of actual to potential GNP. AQ\i is the profit share described in the text, lagged i quarters. Real GNP growth was used as an instrument for %ch(JQM). * denotes significance at the 95% level. ** denotes significance at the 99% level. All regressions were estimated using quarterly data for 1952:4 to 1988:2. Figures in parentheses are standard errors.

Table 1.7 shows the results obtained by adding a second-degree fourth order polynomial of the ratio of actual to potential GNP to equation (1.18).[21] The sum of coefficients is significantly positive at the 97.5% level, while the sum of coefficients on lagged profits is no longer significant at the 95% level. According to this test, part of the

Table 1.8
Effect of Profits on Labor Demand, Controlling for the Ratio of Actual
to Potential GNP: Annual Data

Constant	-10.1	-11.2
	(6.5)	(6.5)
%ch(GDP82)	0.84**	0.84**
	(0.05)	(0.05)
%ch(LM\1)	0.09*	0.07
	(0.05)	(0.05)
GNPRATIO\1	8.4	7.0
	(6.8)	(6.8)
AQ\1		23.1
		(17.1)

Notes: The dependent variable, %ch(LM), is the percent growth in worker hours in manufacturing. %ch(GDP82) is the percentage change in real manufacturing GDP. %ch(LM\1) is %ch(LM), lagged one quarter. GNPRATIO\1 is the lagged ratio of actual to potential GNP. AQ\1 is the first lag of the profit share variable described in the text. Real GNP growth was used as an instrument for %ch(GDP82). * denotes significance at the 95% level. ** denotes significance at the 99% level. Both regressions were estimated using annual data for 1950 to 1987. Figures in parentheses are standard errors.

profits result is a cyclical phenomenon. Most of the profits effect remains, however—the sum of coefficients is still 80.3, compared with 143.4 in the base case (the final column of Table 1.1).

The significance of the relative GNP variable, however, is sensitive to the specification of the equation. When real GNP is used as an instrument for manufacturing GDP, the sum of coefficients on the lagged ratio of actual to potential GNP is no longer significant. (Lagged profits, however, are insignificant as well.) In addition, when the equation is estimated using annual data, lagged relative GNP has a t-statistic of only 1.04 (Table 1.8). In fact, at the industry level, not only is the lagged ratio of actual to potential GNP insignificant, but in eight cases the coefficient on lagged profits is larger when the relative GNP measure is present.

The obvious multicollinearity between profits and the ratio of actual to potential GNP make these results difficult to interpret. While the relative GNP variable reduces the size and significance of the profits effect, its own sum of coefficients is significant only for quarterly data, and only when instruments are used for the change in output. When instruments are added or when annual data are used, actual GNP relative to potential is less significant than profits. The conclusion drawn from these results is that the addition of profits to the labor hours equation explains movements in productivity which a more standard measure of the business cycle (the ratio of actual to potential GNP) cannot.

Robert Gordon has suggested that firms "tend to consistently hire more workers in the last stages of a business expansion than is justified by the level of output."[22] This does not fit nicely into the theoretical framework of Section 2, and in fact Gordon used an ad hoc framework. He labeled his empirical finding the "end-of-expansion" phenomenon. Since profits may simply be proxying for this effect, Gordon's variable was added to the profits regression.

In Gordon's 1979 paper, the variable "EOE" was constructed to take positive values for the six quarters following the cyclical peak in the ratio of actual GNP to potential GNP, and negative values for the next eight quarters.[23] (In his 1993 article, Gordon altered the definition of his EOE variable, but it was still similar to the original.)[24] This variable differs conceptually from the ratio of actual to potential GNP in that it is related specifically to the timing of the business cycle, whereas the relative GNP variable depends more directly on the level of output. For the recession of 1957-58, Gordon used four positive and six negative quarters, claiming that business cycles in the 1950s moved more quickly than they do now. My larger sample includes the recessions of 1953-54, 1980, and 1981-82. Given the relative brevity of the first two of these recessions, they fall into the 4,6 category. (In his 1993 paper, Gordon excluded the 1960 and 1980 recessions.) Gordon set the values of the dummy variable such that they sum to zero over the business cycle. In addition, each business cycle was given equal weight.

We expect this variable to have a positive coefficient—the positive values of EOE at the end of the expansion should be correlated with the buildup of excess labor hours, while its negative values coincide with the gradual dissipation of the excess. When EOE is included in equation (1.18), it has a positive coefficient (Table 1.9), significant at the 99% level, but the sum of coefficients on the profit share is nearly unchanged. The same result holds when instruments are used for the change in output.

Table 1.9
Effect of Profits on Labor Demand, Controlling for Gordon's End-of-
Expansion Effect

Constant	-1.81**	-5.97**	-1.74**	-5.21**
	(0.22)	(1.41)	(0.22)	(1.46)
%ch(JQM)	0.52**	0.51**	0.64**	0.66**
	(0.03)	(0.03)	(0.03)	(0.03)
%ch(JMHM\1)	0.28**	0.27**	0.22**	0.19**
	(0.03)	(0.04)	(0.03)	(0.04)
EY	0.14**	0.19**		
	(0.05)	(0.05)		
EOE	5.52**	5.19**	5.90**	5.42**
	(1.72)	(1.68)	(1.82)	(1.82)
AQ\1		26.1		31.5
		(91.4)		(97.7)
AQ\2		108.7		83.7
		(91.7)		(97.1)
Sum of		134.8**		115.2**
lagged AQ		(45.3)		(47.4)
Instrument for %ch(JQM)	no	no	yes	yes

Notes: The dependent variable is %ch(JMHM), the annual rate of change in the index of hours for manufacturing. %ch(JQM) is the annual rate of change in real manufacturing output. %ch(JMHM\1) is %ch(JMHM) lagged one quarter. EY is the forecasted rate of change in real manufacturing output for the following quarter. EOE is Gordon's end-of-expansion variable. AQ\i is the profit share described in the text, lagged i quarters. Real GNP growth was used as an instrument for %ch(JQM). * denotes significance at the 95% level. ** denotes significance at the 99% level. All regressions were estimated using quarterly data for 1952:4 to 1988:2. Figures in parentheses are standard errors.

Dickens modified Gordon's test in order to argue that recessions permanently lower the level of labor productivity.[25] This conficts with my hypothesis, since during recessions, the profit share is low, implying that productivity should be permanently higher, not lower. Dickens based his conclusion on a variable (called "DOWN" in this chapter) which is positive when Gordon's variable is positive, but zero otherwise. With labor productivity as the dependent variable, he found that this variable has a negative coefficient, meaning that the ending of an expansion permanently raises labor requirements.

The problem with his result is that the rest of the equation he estimated was misspecified. The equation Dickens estimated is:

(1.19)
$$\Delta(Y_t - L_t) = C0 + C1*EOE_t + C2*DOWN_t$$
$$+ C3*DUMMY1_t + C4*DUMMY2_t + e'_t,$$

where the dummies are defined similarly to the slowdown dummies used in Table 1.1. If, instead, we solve equation (1.14) for Dickens' dependent variable, remove expected output, and include slowdown dummies and Gordon's EOE, we have

(1.20)
$$\Delta(Y_t - L_t) = \beta_1 \Delta Y_t - \beta_1 \Delta L_{t-1} + (1-\beta_1)z' + C1*EOE_t$$
$$+ C3*DUMMY1_t + C4*DUMMY2_t + e'_t.$$

where $e'_t = (1-\beta_1)e_t$. Comparing this with Dickens' equation for labor productivity growth, we can see that Dickens left out both the contemporaneous change in output and the lagged change in labor hours. Basically, he treated EOE as a control for the effects of the business cycle, when in fact Gordon only meant it as an enhancement of the effects of the business cycle. (Gordon included output growth in his regressions.) By construction, Dickens' DOWN variable proxies for periods when output is falling, so its negative coefficient is not surprising.

(Dickens has argued that the presence of ΔY as a dependent variable introduces a simultaneity problem, because high productivity growth rates in the long run cause high output growth rates. I am not convinced that this is sufficient reason for excluding output growth from the labor hours equation. Neither were Allen and Link, who rebutted Dickens on this point.[26])

With hours as the dependent variable, Dickens' result holds if DOWN has a positive coefficient. When equation (1.20) is estimated with lagged profit share and DOWN included among the independent variables, Dickens' variable does indeed have a positive coefficient, but neither it nor Gordon's variable are significant (Table 1.10). The sum of coefficients on profits, however, is unchanged.

At least partly because of procyclical productivity, the profit share tends to be highest during recoveries, and lowest while output is declining in a recession. On the other hand, unemployment tends to be high late in a recession and low in the final stages of a recovery. Thus, the profit share tends to be inversely correlated with the unemployment rate. It is possible that we are mistaking an unemployment-induced productivity effect for a profit-induced one. In fact, the theory of the efficiency wage provides a reason why

Table 1.10

Effect of Profits on Labor Demand, Controlling for Gordon's End-of-Expansion Effect, With Dickens' Modification

Constant	-6.38**	-6.44**
	(1.50)	(1.65)
%ch(JQM)	0.52**	0.69**
	(0.03)	(0.04)
%ch(JMHM\1)	0.28**	0.19**
	(0.04)	(0.04)
EY	0.19**	
	(0.05)	
EOE	2.78	-0.54
	(3.38)	(3.74)
DOWN	4.21	10.72*
	(5.13)	(5.95)
AQ\1	24.5	24.2
	(91.5)	(99.3)
AQ\2	117.4	113.7
	(92.4)	(100.3)
Sum of	141.9**	137.9**
lagged AQ	(46.2)	(50.1)
Instrument for %ch(JQM)	no	yes

Notes: The dependent variable is %ch(JMHM), the annual rate of change in the index of manufacturing hours. %ch(JQM) is the annual rate of change in real manufacturing output. %ch(JMHM\1) is %ch(JMHM) lagged one quarter. EY is the forecasted rate of change in real manufacturing output for the following quarter. EOE is Gordon's end-of-expansion variable. DOWN is Dickens' variable, described in the text. AQ\i is the profit share described in the text, lagged i quarters. Real GNP growth was used as an instrument for %ch(JQM). * denotes significance at the 95% level. ** denotes significance at the 99% level. Both regressions were estimated using quarterly data from 1952:4 to 1988:2. Figures in parentheses are standard errors.

unemployment might influence productivity. The efficiency wage model says that the firm pays its workers enough so that being fired as the result of being caught shirking is enough to prevent shirking. The cost of being fired, in turn, is strongly related to the unemployment rate, which proxies for the difficulty of finding other jobs.[27] Under this theory, the higher the unemployment rate, the lower the necessary wage.

Although the theory is normally used to explain wage behavior, it is implicitly a theory of productivity. A high unemployment rate, ceteris paribus, causes workers to work harder to avoid being caught shirking, lowering the labor requirement per unit of output. An

Table 1.11
Effect of Profits on Labor Demand, Controlling for the Efficiency
Wage Theory

Constant	-1.45**	-4.88**	-1.58**	-4.74**
	(0.26)	(1.52)	(0.31)	(1.63)
%ch(JQM)	0.49**	0.48**	0.63**	0.64**
	(0.04)	(0.04)	(0.06)	(0.06)
%ch(JMHM\1)	0.16**	0.18**	0.13**	0.13*
	(0.05)	(0.05)	(0.05)	(0.05)
EY	0.11*	0.14**		
	(0.06)	(0.06)		
ΔRU	-1.41*	-1.45*	0.28	0.33
	(0.84)	(0.84)	(1.33)	(1.36)
ΔRU\1	-1.58**	-1.41*	-1.97**	-1.87**
	(0.65)	(0.66)	(0.68)	(0.68)
ΔRU\2	-0.62	-0.39	-0.82*	-0.62
	(0.36)	(0.37)	(0.41)	(0.42)
ΔRU\3	0.16	0.36	0.62	0.87
	(0.52)	(0.52)	(0.51)	(0.53)
ΔRU\4	-0.56	-0.42	-0.73	-0.60
	(0.53)	(0.53)	(0.56)	(0.57)
Sum of ΔRU\i	-4.01**	-3.33**	-2.63**	-1.89
	(1.18)	(1.21)	(1.41)	(1.51)
AQ\1		-33.0		-8.8
		(97.0)		(103.7)
AQ\2		144.8		113.3
		(98.9)		(104.2)
Sum of lagged AQ		111.8*		104.5*
		(48.6)		(51.3)
Instrument for %ch(JQM)	no	no	yes	yes

Notes: The dependent variable is %ch(JMHM), the annual rate of change in the index of manufacturing hours. %ch(JQM) is the annual rate of change in real manufacturing output. %ch(JMHM\1) is %ch(JMHM) lagged one quarter. EY is the forecasted rate of change in real manufacturing output for the following quarter. ΔRU\i is the ith lag of the change in the unemployment rate for men aged 25 to 54. AQ\i is the profit share described in the text, lagged i quarters. Real GNP growth was used as an instrument for %ch(JQM). * denotes significance at the 95% level. ** denotes significance at the 99% level. All regressions were estimated using quarterly data for 1952:4 to 1988:2. Figures in parentheses are standard errors.

increase in the unemployment rate can be incorporated into the model of Section 2 as a reduction in X, the difficulty of obtaining effort from workers. If this implication of the efficiency wage theory is correct, changes in the unemployment rate should have a negative coefficient in the labor demand equation. Sachs offered an alternative explanation for the same result—when unemployment is high, firms face less opposition from unions and workers towards efforts to make production more efficient.[28]

To test the impact of efficiency wage behavior on productivity growth, we need a measure of labor market slack which is not affected by the changing composition of the labor force during the postwar period. The first difference of the unemployment rate for married men, spouse present, was used. A third degree PDL of the current value and four lags of the variable was added to the hours equation (1.18).[29] Due to possible simultaneity (falling manufacturing employment raises the aggregate unemployment rate, as long as short run employment changes in other sectors are not inversely correlated with those in manufacturing), this coefficient will be biased away from zero.

The sum of coefficients on the rate of change of unemployment variables are indeed significant at the 99% level, and the significance of the profits effect falls slightly (Table 1.11). Evidence of strong simultaneity, however, is provided by the reduction in the sum of the coefficients on current and expected output and lagged labor hours from 0.96 to 0.80. When I use instruments for the change in output, the sum of coefficients on the unemployment rate is cut from −3.3 to −1.9 and becomes statistically insignificant, but lagged profits are still significant at the 97.5% level.

Regressions using annual data (Table 1.12), both for aggregate manufacturing and for two-digit industries, yield similar results. I conclude that low profits are not proxying for high unemployment or the ability of firms to get workers to work harder when unemployment is high.

Finally, it has been suggested that the apparent result that productivity rises when profits fall is due to the fact that when profits fall, firms shut down their least efficient facilities, or that inefficient firms fail.[30] Blanchard and Diamond showed that hirings tend to be spread out over time, while layoffs come in bunches, and argued that recessions are times of "cleaning up" excess labor.[31] The profits effect that I have identified, however, should not be confused with the idea

Table 1.12
Effect of Profits on Labor Demand, Controlling for the Efficiency
Wage Theory: Annual Data

Constant	-1.3*	-3.9*
	(0.6)	(1.7)
%ch(GDP82)	0.60**	0.58**
	(0.13)	(0.13)
%ch(LM\1)	0.06	0.03
	(0.05)	(0.05)
ΔRU	-1.18*	-1.31*
	(0.68)	(0.65)
AQ\1		26.1
		(15.4)

Notes: The dependent variable, %ch(LM), is the percent growth in worker hours in manufacturing. %ch(GDP82) is the percentage change in real manufacturing GDP. %ch(LM\1) is %ch(LM), lagged one quarter. ΔRU is the change in the unemployment rate for married men aged 25 to 54. AQ\1 is the first lag of the profit share variable described in the text. Real GNP growth was used as an instrument for %ch(GDP82). * denotes significance at the 95% level. ** denotes significance at the 99% level. Both regressions were estimated using annual data from 1950 to 1987. Figures in parentheses are standard errors.

that when firms cut back output, they close down their least efficient plants. In such cases, productivity gains are tied to lower output, not to lower profits. In fact, the models of Sections 7 and 8 suggest that the threat of bankruptcy or the closing down of a plant is at least as important as the actual plant closing, since the threat is what compels management and labor to boost productivity. Finally, data analyzed by Davis and Haltiwanger show that the proportion of job destruction due to plant closings actually decreases slightly in recessions.[32]

4. CYCLICAL AND NONCYCLICAL COMPONENTS OF PROFITS

A useful first step in determining the source of the profits-productivity link is to separate profits into its cyclical and noncyclical components, and to substitute these pieces in place of total profits in the labor hours equation. The literature suggests at least two possible ways to do this. In one method, Peter Clark, using NIPA profits, divided pretax output minus profits into four income-side components:

labor costs, depreciation, net business taxes and net interest.[33] Cyclical movements in these variables' share of output leave cyclical movements in profits' share of output as a residual. To derive a cyclical profit share series, Clark then made certain assumptions about how the four variables should move with output. Given that I focus on accounting rather than on NIPA profits, and given the problems inherent in making the required assumptions about how the income shares behave, this approach was not used.

A second way to decompose the profit share into cyclical and noncyclical components, utilized by Feldstein and Summers and in this study, is simply to regress the profit rate on certain cyclical variables, using fitted values from this regression as the cyclical component of the profit share and the residuals as the noncyclical component.[34] As the cyclical variable, I used the Federal Reserve Board's capacity utilization rate, as did Feldstein and Summers.

Two variables not included in the Feldstein-Summers regressions were added here to correct for profits movements which might otherwise be wrongly interpreted as cyclical. The first of these is the rate of change of prices. Inflation reduces the real value of depreciation allowances and boosts nominal capital gains on inventories and other assets, and thus raises accounting profits, ceteris paribus. The second additional variable included here is a dummy variable for 1974 to the present, the period after the first OPEC shock. The main reason for doing this is to capture any differences in the relationship between profits and its determinants between the two time periods. Another reason for including this variable is that the definition of accounting profits changed somewhat in 1974.

Although my analysis of cyclical productivity suggests that the rate of change of output might also be included, the addition of its first lag to the labor hours equation (lagged because profits are lagged) causes multicollinearity problems with the change in lagged labor hours already present in the equation. For both aggregate manufacturing and for several two-digit industries, the sum of coefficients on output and lagged labor hours in the labor hours equations drops well below one with this variable in the profits equation. In several cases, lagged labor hours take a negative coefficient because much of what is simply lagged adjustment of labor hours to high output appears to be caused by high lagged cyclical

Table 1.13

Effect of Cyclical and Noncyclical Components of Profits on Labor Demand

Constant	-21.9**	-12.0*
	(3.8)	(5.9)
%ch(JQM)	0.50**	0.62**
	(0.03)	(0.03)
%ch(JMHM\1)	0.26**	0.21**
	(0.03)	(0.04)
EY	0.26**	
	(0.05)	
AQCYC\1	454.4**	172.9*
+AQCYC\2	(89.2)	(84.4)
AQNONCYC\1	134.9**	74.7
+AQNONCYC\2	(42.8)	(45.8)
Instrument for %ch(JQM)	no	yes

Notes: The dependent variable is %ch(JMHM), the annual rate of change in the index of hours in manufacturing. %ch(JQM) is the annual rate of change in real manufacturing output. %ch(JMHM\1) is %ch(JMHM) lagged one quarter. EY is the forecasted rate of change in real manufacturing output for the following quarter. AQCYC\i is the ith lag of the cyclical component of the profit share, AQ. AQNONCYC\i is the ith lag of the noncyclical component of the profit share, AQ. The equations were estimated simultaneously with the profit share equation. * denotes significance at the 95% level. ** denotes significance at the 99% level. Both regressions were estimated using quarterly data for 1952:4 to 1988:2. Figures in parentheses are standard errors.

profits, due to the correlation between the output change instrument for profits and lagged changes in labor hours.

To obtain correct t-statistics on the cyclical and noncyclical components of lagged profits, the labor hours equation and the profits equation are estimated simultaneously. Cyclical profits are defined as the capacity utilization rate times its coefficient in the profits equation. Noncyclical profits are the residual. To simplify calculations of standard errors, each of the two lags of cyclical profits were constrained to have the same coefficient, as were the two lags of noncyclical profits. The results are shown in Table 1.13.

In the case where the expected future change in output is included in the labor hours equation, both cyclical and noncyclical components of profits are significant at the 99% level. The coefficient on the cyclical part is more than three times the size of the coefficient on the noncyclical part, and more significant. The coefficient on the

Table 1.14

Effect of Cyclical and Noncyclical Components of Lagged Profits on Labor Demand, by Industry

	Textiles (22)	Paper (26)	Chemicals (28)	Petroleum (29)
Constant	-23.0	-12.4	-25.1	incorrect
	(33.7)	(31.1)	(22.5)	
%ch(GDP82)	0.94**	0.54**	0.67**	sign on
	(0.21)	(0.10)	(0.13)	
%ch(L\1)	-0.21	0.18	0.53*	capacity
	(0.30)	(0.23)	(0.28)	
AQCYC\1	76.5	112.1	217.6	utilization
	(131.2)	(351.0)	(382.8)	
AQNONCYC\1	20.8	10.3	45.9*	coefficient
	(71.2)	(21.4)	(20.9)	

	Stone, Clay and Glass (32)	Primary Metals (33)	Fabricated Metals (34)	Nonelectrical Machinery (35)
Constant	-3.1	4.9	-15.0	-189.8
	(2.2)	(16.4)	(9.2)	(127.1)
%ch(GDP82)	0.82**	0.73**	0.99**	1.75**
	(0.06)	(0.05)	(0.05)	(0.66)
%ch(L\1)	0.21**	0.01	0.03	-1.16
	(0.07)	(0.14)	(0.08)	(0.88)
AQCYC\1	11.1	-13.7	101.8	2585
	(12.7)	(48.7)	(65.1)	(2359)
AQNONCYC\1	9.8	9.8	33.8	107
	(18.4)	(14.9)	(20.5)	(102)

	Electrical Machinery (36)	Motor Vehicles (371)	Other Transportation (372@9)	Manufacturing except SIC 29
Constant	-20.0	0.2	incorrect	-19.7*
	(20.6)	(12.0)		(9.7)
%ch(GDP82)	0.95**	0.64**	sign on	0.88**
	(0.10)	(0.06)		(0.05)
%ch(L\1)	-0.18	0.11	capacity	-0.01
	(0.17)	(0.08)		(0.08)
AQCYC\1	342.6	-11.3	utilization	121.7*
	(492.2)	(40.9)		(72.1)
AQNONCYC\1	17.8	-6.1	coefficient	26.7
	(40.6)	(20.2)		(16.3)

Notes on following page.

Notes for Table 1.14: The dependent variable in each case, %ch(L), is the percentage change in the industry's labor hours. %ch(GDP82) is the percent change in each industry's real GDP. %ch(L\1) is %ch(L), lagged one year. AQCYC\1 is the lag of the cyclical component of an industry's profit share, AQ. AQNONCYC\1 is the lag of the noncyclical component of an industry's profit share, AQ. Each equation was estimated simultaneously with the profit share equation. In each case, the percentage change in real GNP was used to instrument for %ch(GDP82). * denotes significance at the 95% level. ** denotes significance at the 99% level. All regressions were estimated using annual data for 1950 to 1987. Figures in parentheses are industry SIC codes or standard errors, where applicable.

noncyclical component, however, is closer to the coefficient on total profits.

In the case where expectations of future output changes are excluded and output is instrumented for, the same general conclusions hold, but the coefficients are less significant. The cyclical coefficient is significant at only the 95% level while the noncyclical coefficient narrowly misses even this. The coefficient on profits in the simple case where no decomposition is made falls about halfway between the coefficients on cyclical and noncyclical profits.

Using annual data, similar results are obtained. For aggregate manufacturing, the coefficient on cyclical profits is nearly five times as large as the coefficient on noncyclical profits, which is roughly equal in size to the coefficient on total profits in equation (1.18). In spite of the difference in size, the t-statistics for the two coefficients are nearly identical, with cyclical profits being barely significant at the 95% level and noncyclical profits just insignificant.

For individual industries (using annual data), the coefficient of cyclical profits is still larger than that for noncyclical profits, but now noncyclical profits are generally more significant than are cyclical profits (Table 1.14). In six of the ten cases where cyclical profits are well-defined (where capacity utilization has a positive coefficient in the profits equation), the t-statistic for noncyclical profits is larger than that for cyclical profits. Also, noncyclical profits are significant in two cases, while cyclical profits are never significant. Nonetheless, the coefficient on the cyclical component of profits is generally much larger.

Data for other OECD countries provide another means of determining whether the profits-productivity phenomenon is primarily cyclical or not. In addition to the U.S., data are available for all the major concepts in our equations for the U.K., West Germany, Canada and Japan. Unfortunately, no quarterly data is available for most of the

Table 1.15
Effect of Profits on Labor Demand: OECD Data

	U.S. (1962-86)	U.S. (1972-86)	U.K. (1972-86)	West Germany (1972-85)
Constant	-8.7**	-10.0**	-3.1	-0.4
	(2.2)	(2.6)	(4.5)	(2.9)
%ch(GDPR)	0.54**	0.58**	0.41*	0.46**
	(0.06)	(0.07)	(0.22)	(0.13)
%ch(L\1)	0.13	0.12	0.50	0.62**
	(0.11)	(0.11)	(0.36)	(0.22)
AQ\1	48.2**	60.2**	14.1	-5.6
	(15.1)	(19.3)	(28.8)	(17.6)

	Canada (1972-84)	Japan (1972-86)
Constant	-6.9	-0.1
	(19.4)	(2.4)
%ch(GDPR)	0.51**	0.28**
	(0.14)	(0.09)
%ch(L\1)	0.42	0.49**
	(0.35)	(0.16)
AQ\1	15.7	-5.8
	(62.4)	(8.5)

Notes: The dependent variable is %ch(L), the percentage change in labor hours in manufacturing. %ch(GDPR) is the percentage change in real manufacturing GDP. %ch(L\1) is the lagged value of %ch(L). AQ\1 is the first lag of the profit share, defined as the operating surplus in manufacturing divided by manufacturing GDP. The percentage change in aggregate real GDP was used as an instrument for %ch(GDPR). * denotes significance at the 95% level. ** denotes significance at the 99% level. All regressions were estimated using annual data, for the interval indicated. Figures in parentheses are standard errors.

series, and annual data goes back only to 1970, leaving very few degrees of freedom.

Data were generally taken from the OECD National Income Accounts. For all countries except Canada, labor hours were found by multiplying total manufacturing employment from the Accounts by a measure of weekly hours worked in manufacturing from the OECD *Main Economic Indicators*. For Canada, manufacturing employment from the same source was used as the hours measure. The output index is real value added in manufacturing, and real GDP is used as an instrument for it. The profits share variable is the operating surplus in manufacturing divided by manufacturing value added. A measure of accounting profits similar to that used above was not available for other countries.

Results for the labor hours equation for each country are shown in Table 1.15. To provide a basis for comparison with the earlier results, a sample period of 1962 to 1986 was used for the U.S., the only country for which data allowed such a lengthy sample. For both the long and short sample periods, profits adversely affect labor productivity growth in the U.S. at the 99% significance level. For other OECD countries, however, the results are mixed—profits have an adverse effect in the U.K. and Canada, but a positive effect in West Germany and Japan. In no cases are the results statistically significant.

To divide profits into cyclical and noncyclical components, we need something to replace capacity utilization, which is not available for some countries in our sample. Instead, an index of industrial production is available for each country studied. To convert this into a measure of the business cycle, local maxima of the logarithm of industrial production were joined to form a concave function for each country. (Such a concave function exists for these countries because output growth has slowed over time in each one.) My replacement for capacity utilization is thus the difference between the actual logarithm of industrial production and the concave function. This is zero at local maxima of industrial production and negative otherwise. Because the definition of profits used here should be independent of inflation, the change in prices is excluded from the profit share regression. In addition, given the small sample size and the fact that it falls almost entirely after 1973, the post-1973 dummy is also excluded.

Again, the sample period 1962 to 1986 for the U.S. provides a crude comparison with the results appearing in previous sections of the chapter. In contrast with the earlier results, the coefficient on noncyclical profits is twice as large as that on cyclical profits (Table 1.16). Neither are significant, however. Using the shorter sample period, noncyclical profits are significantly positive in both the U.S. and West Germany, insignificantly positive for the U.K. and Canada, and negative in Japan. (Remember that a positive coefficient means that a high profit share boosts the growth rate of labor hours for any level of output.) In contrast, cyclical profits are never significant and have a negative coefficient in both West Germany and Japan.

Table 1.16

Effect of Cyclical and Noncyclical Components of Lagged Profits on Labor Demand: OECD Data

	U.S. (1962-86)	U.S. (1972-86)	U.K. (1972-86)	West Germany (1972-85)
Constant	-13.9	-14.3**	-46.3	-17.8*
	(9.5)	(2.9)	(273.7)	(8.7)
%ch(GDPR)	0.61**	0.60**	0.01	0.21
	(0.18)	(0.07)	(6.71)	(0.22)
%ch(L\1)	0.10	-0.02	-0.38	0.81*
	(0.19)	(0.13)	(8.20)	(0.33)
AQCYC\1	38.5	117.5	18	-130.9
	(59.4)	(83.0)	(445)	(143.3)
AQNONCYC\1	76.4	92.7**	265	90.2*
	(59.7)	(21.0)	(1633)	(49.1)

	Canada (1972-84)	Japan (1972-86)
Constant	-164.5	46.2
	(512.5)	(413.3)
%ch(GDPR)	0.69	0.22
	(0.47)	(3.16)
%ch(L\1)	-1.10	1.88
	(4.76)	(17.55)
AQCYC\1	366	-195
	(1052)	(3722)
AQNONCYC\1	516	-176
	(1624)	(1258)

Notes: The dependent variable is %ch(L), the percentage change in labor hours in manufacturing. %ch(GDPR) is the percentage change in real manufacturing GDP. %ch(L\1) is the lagged value of %ch(L). AQCYC\1 is the lagged value of the cyclical component of the profit share AQ, defined as the operating surplus in manufacturing divided by manufacturing GDP. AQNONCYC\1 is the lagged value of the noncyclical component of AQ. The percentage change in aggregate real GDP was used as an instrument for %ch(GDPR). Each equation was estimated simultaneously with the profit share equation. * denotes significance at the 95% level. ** denotes significance at the 99% level. All regressions were estimated using annual data, for the interval indicated. Figures in parentheses are standard errors.

In summary, the profits-productivity link seems related more to noncyclical than to cyclical profits. This conclusion follows both from the generally greater significance of noncyclical profits and from the fact that the coefficient on noncyclical profits is closer to that of aggregate profits than is the coefficient on cyclical profits. As we shall see in Section 8 below, this has important implications in determining the source of the profits-productivity relationship.

5. PAST RESEARCH: THE LITERATURE ON "SATISFICING"

The literature on "satisficing" provides a useful starting point for the bankruptcy model developed in Section 7. Other than Simon's seminal work, however, these models can only explain temporary increases in productivity. Since profits appear to have a permanent effect on the level of productivity, Section 7 revises the models somewhat.

According to Herbert Simon, humans do not naturally "maximize." Rather, "in most psychological theories the motive to act stems from drives, and action terminates when the drive is satisfied." A business sets as its goal a certain level or rate of profit, a certain share of the market, or some level of sales. "When performance falls short of the level of aspiration, search behavior . . . is induced." This search is for, among other things, more efficient methods of production.[35] Thus, a level of profits below the "aspiration level" generates greater productivity. Because increased productivity would result from a shift in the technology of production rather than from an increase in effort, these changes in productivity would be permanent.

Cyert and March, elaborating on Simon's theory, quoted an example from a study by M. W. Reder. Ford Motor Company, after losses of $50 million in the first three quarters of 1946, "'announced that it had found methods of reducing operating costs (on a given volume of output) by about twenty million dollars per year.'"[36]

Harvey Leibenstein presented a theory similar to Simon's. He argued that explicit or implicit contracts between principals and agents specify penalties for an agent's failure to meet minimal standards, but no reward for exceeding those standards. When profits fall below "minimal standards," which Leibenstein did not define, those in authority must exert effort in order to change the effort choices of those beneath them. Workers will change their effort level for two reasons: (1) to avoid undue pressure from superiors; (2) to satisfy the "superego's" desires to fulfil internal standards, which are partly determined by the demands made by one's boss. In Leibenstein's model, however, effort would return to its old levels when the profit share did.[37]

Oliver Williamson set out these ideas in a model. Managers maximize utility, which depends on: (1) salary; (2) staff; (3) discretionary spending for investments on pet projects (those which a purely profit maximizing firm would not undertake); and (4) management "slack" absorbed as cost. This last component consists of expense accounts, office modernization, and the like. (Williamson called these "emoluments"). Williamson cited one case where an office modernization program was launched "with the objective of 'bringing the year's earnings into line and [to] avoid spoiling the stockholders.'" Because salary is related to the amount of staff one has, salary is subsumed under the staff term.[38]

Utility is maximized subject to a satisficing constraint: reported profits must be at least as large as the minimum profits demanded by stockholders. Minimum profits were defined by Williamson to include the amount that a profit maximizing firm would put toward investment. The difference between reported profits and minimum profits goes toward discretionary investment. The difference between the maximum profits possible and reported profits is composed of superfluous staff and slack absorbed as cost. Williamson showed that production itself nonetheless takes place efficiently, i.e., marginal cost equals marginal revenue. As the state of the economy becomes more difficult and output declines, reported profits fall, triggering a reduction in discretionary investment, staff, and emoluments. In percentage terms, the drop in reported profits will be much larger than the reduction in output, so discretionary investment, staff and emoluments decline faster than output.[39] Because staff contracts more than output declines, labor productivity rises. Because of a lag between the drop in profits and the contraction in staff, low profits lead increases in productivity.

Later, Williamson reported several case studies attempting to support his theory empirically. A certain chemical firm had enjoyed rapid growth in sales through the mid-1950s. When growth stagnated in the 1958 recession, the profit/sales ratio dropped from 18% to 9% between 1956 and 1958. When a 16% increase in sales in 1959 failed to revive profits, a new president was appointed in June 1960, and top management was overturned. Within nine months (but not immediately), 20% of all employees had been laid off. Within two years, 20% of hourly, 32% of salaried, and 41% of headquarters employment had been trimmed. In addition, emoluments were reduced. Williamson claimed that adverse demand produced the decline in production employment, while satisficing behavior explains the reduction in salaried employees (staff).[40]

In the case of "Midwest Processing Corp.," profits also fell in the late 1950s. Costs were not reined in until a control budget for headquarters was introduced in January 1961. The chief budgeting officer observed that staff has a tendency to expand unless subjected to careful review. In the case of "General Manufacturing Co.," a large conglomerate, the individual divisions were studied. Five divisions exhibited "extreme conformance" to the model, i.e., staff expense moved in the opposite direction of sales, but were consistent with the profit level. Two divisions contradicted the model.[41]

In the earlier article, Williamson cited some other examples of satisficing behavior. In one case, a firm "under pressure" was "able to reduce its production control staff from 500 to 350 over a weekend without serious difficulty." In another, ". . . a large paper manufacturer has cut its office force by 32 per cent and reduced total overhead by $14 million (on sales of about $180 million) as part of a vigorous cost reduction program."[42]

Although Williamson's theory seems to explain the behavior of staff employment rather well, it disagrees with the empirical evidence. Employment of production workers, as well as that of staff, responds positively to high levels of profits. When the labor demand equation is run using production worker hours, rather than total hours, as the dependent variable, the coefficient of lagged profits is still significantly positive. While this coefficient is somewhat smaller than that for the total labor hours equation, it is still large. Therefore, a theory that has profits affecting only non-production worker hours is insufficient.

In fact, Williamson himself provided some evidence that production worker hours are also affected. A chief budgeting officer of "General Manufacturing Co.," when asked to comment on the statement ". . . when the division encounters adversity and profit goals are not being met, reductions in the levels of indirect costs are usually needed in order to restore profitable performance," responded "Direct costs get closer attention too." In addition, Williamson cited a survey of 200 presidents of leading corporations in a 1961 issue of "Dun's Review and Modern Industry," in which those questioned were most likely to say that cost cutting efforts in their firms focused on production.[43] Therefore, we need a model in which low profits induce cost-cutting across the board.

Another part of the satisficing literature which conflicts with the empirical evidence from the second section of this chapter is Simon's idea that the aspiration level may adjust over time. If this is true, it is the relative, rather than the absolute, aspiration level which will determine productivity growth. Substituting "profit share" for "aspiration level," this says that it is profits relative to their long-run average, rather than absolute profits, which matter. Empirically, this would imply that the sum of the coefficients on lagged profits should sum to zero, since only a change in profits, rather than its level, would affect productivity. In fact, however, this is not the case, so this part of the satisficing theory must be rejected. The bankruptcy model, by fixing the aspiration level, avoids this problem.

6. TIME ALLOCATION MODEL

It is often observed that the installation of new managers results in increased efficiency and a paring-down of unneeded employees. If the new manager is unambiguously better than the old, however, why wait until a profit squeeze to replace the old manager? The firm could replace such a manager anytime. Assuming the firm's goal is to maximize profits, there must be some way in which the old manager was superior to the new one.

One explanation, examined in this section, is that some managers are better at cutting costs, while others are better at increasing market share. When profits per sale are low, the former replace the latter. Alternatively, the same effect of profit share on productivity would obtain if managers concentrate on different tasks given different profit situations. For example, according to Kilby, an International Labor Organization study reported "that low productivity is frequently caused by top management's concern with the commercial and financial affairs of the firm rather than with the running of the factory."[44] In addition, 90% of the panelists involved in the survey described in Williamson agreed with the statement: "The incentives for careful policing [of costs] begin to erode when the pinch eases."[45] While this latter quote is consistent with the bankruptcy model to be presented in Section 7, it is also compatible with a model in which time is diverted toward cost-cutting during recessions, and towards building market share during booms.

The basic outline of the model examined in this section is quite simple. Total profits are the product of sales and profits per sale. When profits per sale are low, the value of an extra sale is low. In such a case, the most effective way to increase profits is by increasing profits per sale. When profits per sale are large, however, profits are boosted more by engaging in non-price competition (e.g., quality improvements, more advertising, better customer service) to increase sales than by increasing profits per sale still further.

Of course, non-price competition increases both sales and profits per sale, by shifting the demand curve out. To the extent that non-price competition raises profits per sale, it thus has the same effect as cutting costs. To simplify the analysis, such effects of non-price competition are ignored.

This section presents two models based on this theory. In the first, a limited supply of time is allocated by a manager between cost-cutting (p) and non-price competition (s). The manager desires only to maximize the profits of the firm. Labor productivity is a function of time spent cutting costs. In equilibrium, as the level of profits increase, time is shifted from cost-cutting to non-price competition, i.e., dp/d(profits) is negative. The second model shows that the firm's optimal decision whether to retain a manager with given cost-cutting and non-price competition abilities depends on the profit share.

To analyze the manager's decision on how to allocate time, I use a two-period model. The manager's time in period 2 is allocated between cost-cutting and non-price competition based on the sales and profits per sale of the firm during period 1. (I assume the manager has no additional information during period 2 about sales or profits in period 2.) The allocation of time in period 2 has its effect on profits during period 2.

This model is somewhat similar to one outlined by Robert Hall, in which a limited amount of labor is allocated between production and the creation of "organizational capital." Hall defined organizational capital as being high when a firm's heterogeneous resources are matched with each other in a way that achieves a high level of output. In Hall's model, however, unlike this model, the allocation of time between production and investment in organizational capital is determined by the real interest rate.[46]

In my model, the firm desires to

$$\underset{s_2, p_2}{\text{Max}} \quad \pi_2 = P_2 S_2 \qquad \text{s.t.} \ T_2 \geq s_2 + p_2$$

where π = profits, P = profits per sale, S = sales, T = total time available to managers, s = time devoted to sales-increasing (non-price competition) activities, and p = time devoted to profit margin-increasing (cost-cutting) activities. Subscripts denote the time period. I also assume that $S_2 = S_2(s_2, S_1)$ and $P_2 = P_2(p_2, P_1)$. That is, both sales and profits per sale depend on their lagged values and on the time spent increasing them during the current period. $\partial S_2 / \partial s_2$, $\partial S_2 / \partial S_1$, $\partial P_2 / \partial p_2$ and $\partial P_2 / \partial P_1$ are all positive. The two types of activities show decreasing returns, i.e., $\partial^2 S_2 / \partial s_2^2 < 0$ and $\partial^2 P_2 / \partial p_2^2 < 0$. Also, to simplify the math, I assume that the marginal impact of period 1's profits per sale on period 2's profits per sale is unaffected by time devoted to sales-increasing activities in period 2, or $\partial^2 P_2 / (\partial p_2 \partial P_1) = 0$.

From the first order conditions, we find that:

$$(1.21) \quad \frac{\partial S_2(s_2, S_1)}{\partial s_2} P_2 = \frac{\partial P_2(p_2, P_1)}{\partial p_2} S_2.$$

Given S_1 and P_1, this equation can be used to determine equilibrium s_2 and p_2. A graphical representation (Chart 1.3) shows the result most clearly. An increase in time spent increasing sales (s_2) reduces $(\partial S_2 / \partial s_2)P_2$, the marginal revenue product of time spent increasing sales, because of decreasing returns. As a function of s_2, $(\partial S_2/\partial s_2)P_2$ is therefore downward sloping. By a similar argument, the marginal revenue product of time spent cutting costs, $(\partial P_2/\partial p_2)S_2$, is downward sloping in p_2, time spent cutting costs. The intersection of the two marginal revenue curves produces equilibrium at point E.

An increase in lagged profits per sale, P_1, boosts current period profits per sale, P_2, thus increasing the return to activities which increase sales. In Chart 1.3, this causes an upward shift of the $(\partial S/\partial s)P$ curve, to $(\partial S_2/\partial s_2)P_2'$. The firm devotes more resources to sales-increasing activities and fewer to cost-cutting activites, shifting the equilibrium to the point E'. (The assumption that $\partial^2 P_2/(\partial p_2 \partial P_1) = 0$ means that the curve representing the marginal revenue product of

Chart 1.3
Equilibrium Allocation of Time Between Cost-Cutting and Sales-Increasing Activities

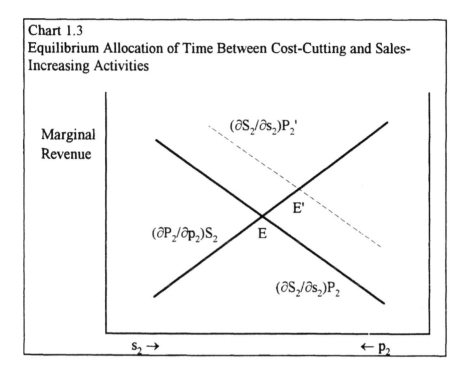

cost-cutting does not move.) This is the desired result: higher profits in period 1 cause cost-cutting activities in period 2 to be diminished. A rigorous mathematical treatment of this result is contained in Appendix B.

The corollary to this result is that $ds_2/dP_1 > 0$, i.e., that if lagged profits are high, managers devote a large amount of time to non-price competition. This means that more effort is devoted to advertising, sales, better customer service, and the like. The model thus explains rather well Williamson's observation that high profits lead to a proliferation of staff (which is engaged chiefly in what this chapter terms "non-price competition"). At the same time, the model deals with the lack of production worker cost-cutting in the satisficing models by broadening cost-cutting to cover all workers.

Extending the result to a multi-period context is complicated by the feedback effects of p_2 and s_2 on subsequent P and S, and thus on subsequent p and s. For example, an increase in p_2, the amount of time during period 2 spent cutting costs, will push up P_2, thus making s, time spent raising sales, more valuable in subsequent periods. The resulting decline in p in those periods must be taken account of when determining p_2. The result should be that p_2 still moves in the same direction it would have in the two-period model, but by a larger or smaller amount.

The second model of this section explains why firms switch to managers who are better at cutting costs when profitability falls. When profits increase, on the other hand, managers with a comparative advantage at non-price competition will be chosen to replace those who are better at cutting costs. The model shows that when such managers are hired, the amount and quality of time spent on cost cutting falls.

Using the same timing framework and notation as in the first model, $S_2 = S_2(A_j s_2, S_1)$ and $P_2 = P_2(p_2/A_j, P_1)$, where A_j is manager j's relative ability at sales-increasing activities. This means that as A increases, i.e., as managers with greater ability at sales-increasing activity (higher A) are chosen, sales (S_2) increase, while profits per sale (P_2) fall. What happens to profits when $A_j > A_k$ and manager j replaces manager k? When A_j and A_k are close together, the derivative $d\pi_2/dA$ (= $\partial\pi_2/\partial A$ by the envelope theorem) answers that question:

$$(1.22) \quad \frac{d\pi_2}{dA} = s_2 \frac{\partial S_2}{\partial (As_2)} P_2 - \frac{S_2 P_2}{A^2} \frac{\partial P_2}{\partial p_2} .$$

Because of adjustment costs of changing managers, and because this model ignores other characteristics of managers, we should not expect firms to choose managers such that the condition $d\pi_2/dA = 0$ is always met exactly. In addition, we must assume that the relative salaries of managers with different A are not flexible enough to offset sudden changes in the relative value of cost-cutting or sales-increasing skills. Otherwise, firms would simply match each manager's salary to his or her marginal revenue product at every point in time, meaning no turnover in managers when the relative value of cost-cutting or sales-increasing skills changed.

To determine what types of managers will be dismissed, we must determine what happens to $d\pi_2/dA$, the change in profits from switching to a manager with higher A, when lagged profits, P_1, change. Appendix C shows that, with a few modest assumptions, an increase in lagged profits causes $d\pi_2/dA$ to increase, meaning that firms will switch away from some managers with better cost-cutting abilities. This result follows for two reasons, corresponding to the two terms in equation (1.22). The first is that higher profits per sale in the past raise profits per sale today, making proficiency at non-price competition (sales-increasing activities) more valuable. The second reason for a positive derivative is that, no matter what kind of manager the firm employs, as P_1 increases, there is substitution away from cost-cutting toward non-price competition. Thus, the better a manager is at non-price competition relative to cost-cutting, the more the firm benefits.

As stated above, because of adjustment costs and other factors, a change in $d\pi_2/dA$ does not mean that a particular manager will definitely be replaced or moved. However, in any borderline cases, it does. Large shifts in $d\pi_2/dA$ will imply large scale turnover of managers, and higher or lower productivity.

The models of this section single out non-price competition which is non productivity-improving, such as advertising and sales. In general, these include efforts to differentiate the market which contribute little to consumer utility, but rather serve to take business from one's competitors or to shift the demand curve. Unfortunately, both of the models of this section ignore non-price competition which is productivity-improving: producing more or "better" output with the same quantity of inputs. This non-price competition form of productivity growth will suffer when profits are low—when profitability is low, there is less incentive to innovate, since capturing greater market share is not as lucrative.

Finally, the manager's or firm's reaction to low lagged profits may depend on the reason they are low. To the extent that lagged profits are simply cyclically low, non-price competition, by increasing sales, simultaneously increases profits per sale, because constant fixed costs and sticky labor hours are spread over more sales. In such a case, there would be less reason to prefer cost-cutting, since profits per sale could also be increased through an increase in sales.

7. LIQUIDITY CONSTRAINT MODEL

Several pieces of anecdotal evidence from the early 1980s show that firms are willing to undertake drastic measures to restore profitability when faced with possible bankruptcy. In late 1983, Eastern Airlines, faced with losses since 1980, adopted a cost-cutting program aimed at $75 million per year in "productivity gains." Actual gains totalled $46.5 million. In this case, it was the employees, willing to work harder to save their jobs, who made the concessions.[47]

In another example, GM set up its Saturn Corporation following big losses in the early 1980s and threatened by foreign competition. Again it was the union which was willing to accept work rule changes (although Saturn's employees were not yet hired, thus not yet members of the union) in order to preserve jobs. The Wall Street Journal reported:

> UAW leaders acknowledge that the labor content of U.S.-built autos must be cut substantially to get manufacturing costs down to the level of Japanese imports, and the union is making scattered efforts to do so with GM and other U.S. auto makers. But with Saturn, GM executives and UAW leaders plan to go beyond what they have done so far to cut costs. . . . Fewer work rules would make many jobs more taxing and cut staff levels . . . 'But hopefully Saturn means that not all the small-car jobs will go overseas,' a UAW staff member said."[48]

In addition, some empirical evidence supports the view that the threat of bankruptcy causes greater productivity. Weisskopf, Bowles and Gordon found that "competitive pressure" was statistically significant at improving productivity. They defined competitive pressure as a three-year moving average of the residual from a regression of business failures on capacity utilization, i.e., business failures adjusted for the cycle. The authors also found that a business failure rate unadjusted for the cycle is just as significant.[49] (However, in the discussion of the paper, it was noted that in 1978, 62% of all bankruptcies were in retailing and construction, where turnover rates are high. Given this noise, it is somewhat uncertain what Weisskopf, Bowles and Gordon's variables mean.)

Of course, it is also easy to imagine situations where the threat of bankruptcy reduces productivity. The best workers may look for work in advance of expected layoffs, increasing turnover at the firm and reducing the average quality of the remaining workforce. The fear of being laid off may reduce worker morale. Suppliers, especially suppliers of credit, may be less willing to deal with a firm in financial difficulty. The model presented in this section focuses on the case where the threat of bankruptcy improves productivity. However, it can also incorporate cases where the threat of bankruptcy hurts productivity.

This section presents a liquidity constraint model, the first of two bankruptcy-related explanations of the profits-productivity relationship explored in this chapter. The liquidity constraint hypothesis assumes that bankruptcy will occur if profits during some period fall below a certain level, as Hamermesh assumed.[50] This happens because there is a limit to the amount of borrowing a firm can do over some period of time without encountering resistance from creditors. Low profits will increase the amount which must be borrowed and may be interpreted as a signal for inability to repay. After presenting the model, this section then examines how well some testable implications of the model stack up against industry data.

In both bankruptcy models, workers or managers receive quasi-rents from the firm, i.e., higher pay and more stable employment than if they were forced to look for another job, which cause them to care whether the firm survives. There is thus a tradeoff between the disutility of extra effort—as broadly defined below—of workers as a group (or managers as a group), and the added utility from reducing the probability of bankruptcy through this extra effort. As lagged profits, which help forecast current and future profits, fall, the marginal change in the probability of bankruptcy due to a change in effort is greater. Thus, lower lagged profits stimulate greater effort, increasing productivity in current and future periods.

Before describing either bankruptcy model in detail, the identity of the actor whose behavior is being studied must be clarified. In the case study examples above, only non-managers were seen making sacrifices for their companies, although the model can apply to either managers or non-supervisory workers or to both. It is important, however, that a group, rather than an individual, is involved. This is because no single manager or worker, by changing his or her level of effort or behavior, will have a discernible impact on the firm, and therefore on his or her own future. Thus, we must assume that management as a group or production workers as a group undertake to change their effort. Those who attempt free ridership will be subject to some sort of social sanction by members of the group who have modified their effort. In the case of Eastern or of any unionized firm, this social sanction takes the form of collectively bargained work rule changes. Since the agent we thus model is a group, it is easiest to assume that all members of the group have the same utility function, so that the group can be treated as a representative agent. While this is not essential to the result, it simplifies the model considerably.

I must also define "effort," a vital feature of the model, before we begin. For non-management workers, Leibenstein postulated effort along four dimensions: activity, pace, quality, and time ("APQT"). Workers can vary the activities they choose to undertake (if there is more than one way to do something), their pace of work, the quality of their work (through a change in concentration), and the time pattern of work (irrelevant here other than for piecework).[51]

Since the regressions in Section 2 indicate that a low profit level leads to a permanent shift in the level of productivity, however, it is important that effort be defined as something which permanently increases productivity, rather than something which increases productivity only as long as it lasts. For example, if one says, as does Leibenstein, that worker effort is an increase in the pace at which work is done, then a change in the profit level produces only a temporary change in effort. If, on the other hand, effort means a willingness to accept work rule changes, which become permanent through the tendency for custom to become embedded in behavior, then a low level of profits will lead to permanently higher productivity. Thus, in my bankruptcy models, I focus on "effort" as the willingness to permanently accept more efficient work rules. (This differs from the definition of effort in the second chapter of this study.) To guarantee an equilibrium, I will assume that as effort increases, the marginal disutility of effort increases.

Similarly, if it is the "effort" of managers which matters, effort must be defined so that a temporary increase (in response to temporarily low profits) produces a permanent shift in the level of productivity. An example of managerial effort which does not permanently enhance productivity is greater pressure on or closer monitoring of subordinates. Although a drop in profits may encourage more of this type of behavior, productivity would be higher only while it lasted.

For managers, "psychological disutility" captures my meaning better than "effort." Psychological disutility will vary along several dimensions. In Williamson's work, managers value staff, so that higher productivity through cutting of staff causes managerial disutility. In addition, managers must engage in search in order to find ways to cut costs. Intensification of such search increases effort. Swallowing individual or corporate pride to accept better methods of management is another possible component of psychological disutility.

Finally, to the extent that managers dislike firing people, cost-cutting involves another disagreeable aspect. As with workers, I assume that the marginal disutility of "effort" increases as effort increases.

Model

For simplicity, a two period model similar to that of the last section is used. In period 2, workers (or managers) know only the profit share of period 1 and form expectations based only on information available from period 1. In period 2, effort, other aspects of technology, market demand, factor prices and competitive conditions determine profits. Based on these profits, the bankruptcy decision is made.

The model assumes that the profit share obeys the following relationship:

$$(1.23) \quad \pi_2 = a + b\pi_1 + X + e,$$

where π is profits per dollar of value added, b is a parameter between zero and one, X is effort in period 2, and e is a white noise error in period 2. Effort is normalized to affect profits unit for unit. In this framework, a and b are parameters, X is set by workers, and e is a random variable. Since the firm goes bankrupt if $\pi_2 < W$ (note that I have modified the bankruptcy condition to refer to the profit share rather than the level of profits),[52] we can write

$$(1.24) \quad \begin{aligned} B &= \text{Prob}(\pi_2 < W) = \text{Prob}(a + b\pi_1 + X + e < W) \\ &= \text{Prob}(e < W - a - b\pi_1 - X), \end{aligned}$$

where Prob(z) denotes the probability of z.

Workers' utility (U) is a function of the present discounted value of lifetime income (Y) and "effort," (X):

$$(1.25) \quad U = U(Y, X) \qquad \partial U / \partial Y > 0, \partial U / \partial X < 0.$$

Effort can affect utility in two ways. The first is the direct disutility effect already referred to above. Secondly, effort can affect utility through its impact on income.

In this model, workers cannot influence income directly. Rather, income is a function of the bankruptcy rate, which is in turn affected by effort. (To the extent that an individual's pay is based on that individual's performance, greater effort yields greater income. Since this effect complicates the analysis without adding any insight as to why profits affect productivity growth, I ignore it.) If Y* is expected income given that the firm stays in business for a third period, Y_0 is expected income given that the firm fails immediately after period 2, and B is the probability of failure following period 2, then $\partial Y / \partial B = Y_0 - Y^* < 0$. Workers care about bankruptcy in period 2 because it affects their income in period 3. For all other purposes, however, period 3 can be ignored.

The worker maximizes utility with respect to effort (X):

$$(1.26) \quad \frac{dU(Y,X)}{dX} = \frac{\partial U}{\partial Y} \frac{\partial Y}{\partial B} \frac{\partial B}{\partial X} + \frac{\partial U}{\partial X} = 0.$$

This equation says that in equilibrium, the gain to income through lower risk of bankruptcy exactly offsets the disutility of the extra effort needed to produce the income gain. As shown above, $\partial Y/\partial B$ equals $Y_0 - Y^*$, which is negative. (Although $\partial U/\partial Y$ is decreasing in Y, this fact needlessly complicates the analysis, so I assume $\partial U/\partial Y$ is constant.)

Assuming a positive correlation between effort (X) and productivity, the model shows that an increase in π_1, lagged profits, reduces current effort, thus reducing productivity. A mathematical derivation of this result is given in Appendix D. Since the result can be portrayed more clearly using graphs, however, I follow a graphical approach here.

Equation (1.26) can be rearranged to yield

$$(1.27) \quad \frac{\partial U}{\partial Y} \frac{\partial Y}{\partial B} \frac{\partial B}{\partial X} = -\frac{\partial U}{\partial X}.$$

Because $\partial U/\partial Y$ and $\partial Y/\partial B$ are constants, the variables of interest are $\partial B/\partial X$ and $\partial U/\partial X$. I assume that $\partial U/\partial X$ (which is always negative) slopes downward in X (i.e., $\partial^2 U/\partial X^2 < 0$). That is, as the level of effort increases, extra units have a greater marginal disutility.

To find $\partial B/\partial X$, I assume that e is described by a probability density function with only one local maximum (i.e., one hump). Recall from equation (1.24) that B is the probability that e is less than $W - a - b\pi_1 - X$. B is thus the area below the e curve and to the right of $W - a - b\pi_1 - X$ in Chart 1.4. The chart assumes equilibrium lies to the right of the maximum of e (the other case is explored below). As X increases, $W - a - b\pi_1 - X$ moves farther to the right in the tail, i.e.,

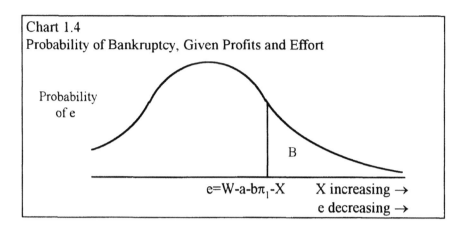

Chart 1.4
Probability of Bankruptcy, Given Profits and Effort

Probability of e

B

$e=W-a-b\pi_1-X$

X increasing $\rightarrow$
e decreasing $\rightarrow$

the probability of bankruptcy declines. This shows that $\partial B/\partial X$ is negative. In fact, $\partial B/\partial X$ is simply the negative of the height of the probability density function for e at $W-a-b\pi_1-X$.

Since $\partial U/\partial Y$ and $\partial Y/\partial B$ are constants, $(\partial U/\partial Y)(\partial Y/\partial B)(\partial B/\partial X)$, the indirect impact on utility of a change in effort, is a linear function of $\partial B/\partial X$, the impact of effort on bankruptcy. Without loss of generality, we can scale utility such that $(\partial U/\partial Y)(\partial Y/\partial B) = -1$, causing the indirect impact on utility of a change in effort to simplify to $-\partial B/\partial X$. But we saw in the last paragraph that $-\partial B/\partial X$ for each X is the pdf of e at $W-a-b\pi_1-X$. The marginal utility of effort in this case is thus the pdf of e (Chart 1.5). Equilibrium, as defined by equation (1.27), is found where this marginal utility of effort curve intersects with the marginal disutility of effort $(-\partial U/\partial X)$ curve. The

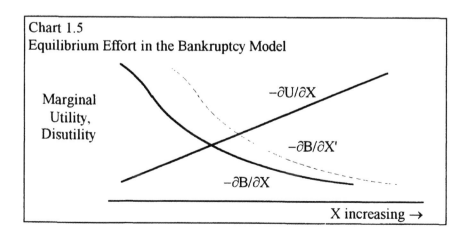

Chart 1.5
Equilibrium Effort in the Bankruptcy Model

Marginal Utility, Disutility

$-\partial U/\partial X$

$-\partial B/\partial X'$

$-\partial B/\partial X$

X increasing $\rightarrow$

marginal utility of greater effort, which raises income by reducing the probability of bankruptcy, thus equals the marginal disutility to the worker or manager of this effort.

In Chart 1.4, a decrease in π_1 boosts $W - a - b\pi_1 - X$, which equals e, and thus moves us to the left along the pdf of e for any given level of effort, X. In Chart 1.5, this is equivalent to an rightward shift of $(\partial U/\partial Y)(\partial Y/\partial B)(\partial B/\partial X)$ to the dashed line $(-\partial B/\partial X')$, since e is higher for any value of X. A drop in profits causes workers or managers to expend more effort, because the reduced profits mean that each additional unit of effort, on the margin, is more important in warding off bankruptcy than when bankruptcy is not really a threat.

In the case where the firm begins to the left of the hump in the pdf of e, it is in a position where avoiding a bankruptcy is so unlikely that workers cannot significantly improve their situation by boosting effort. This is the type of case mentioned at the beginning of this section, in which the threat of bankruptcy reduces productivity by lowering morale. An increase in profits, moving the firm to the right along the pdf, acts as encouragement—the firm has a better shot at making it, so increased effort will help much more.

Empirical Tests

One test of "productivity growth to avoid bankruptcy" models in general is to examine how the profits-productivity relationship responds to differences in the wage premium. Going back to Chart 1.5, one can see that when $\partial Y/\partial B$—the amount of future income lost due to bankruptcy—increases, the downward sloping curve will shift up by a larger amount, causing a larger increase in effort. This is the graphical equivalent of saying that when workers have more to lose, they should be willing to make greater sacrifices. Thus, industries where the potential loss in worker income due to loss of job is greatest are those which should have the biggest increases in productivity when profits are low.

To test this, I assume that the wage premium is a logarithmic function of the wage. That is, I assume that the difference between the current wage and the alternative wage—the expected wage a worker would receive if laid off, adjusted for time spent unemployed—increases with the current wage. My proxy for the wage premium for each industry is thus the average of the logarithm of average hourly earnings over the sample period. If the probability of bankruptcy is a linear function of profits, then the coefficient on profits in the change in labor hours equation (1.18) takes the form $a + \beta W_1$, where W_1 is the average of the logarithm of average hourly earnings for industry i, and a and β are constant over all industries. This expression is imposed on the profits coefficient for each industry by stacking the regressions.

The bankruptcy hypothesis predicts that β will be positive—as the wage (and thus the wage premium) increases, profits will have a larger effect on productivity. In fact, however, β is significantly negative at the 95% level. Although this would seem to contradict the theory, there is an obvious explanation. Industries with high wage premiums, such as steel and motor vehicles, tend to also be the industries with the most volatile profits. In industries accustomed to wide swings in profits, a given change in profits will have less significance for long-term profitability, and thus bring about less of a productivity response. (In terms of equation (1.27), this is represented by a smaller increase in $\partial B/\partial X$ for a given reduction in profits. In Chart 1.4, it would mean fatter tails on the e_t curve.)

The ideal test of the bankruptcy hypothesis would use $\partial B/\partial X$ as an independent variable. Since this is not directly observable, I must use the profit share. One might expect, however, that $\partial B/\partial X$ is not a linear function of profits—a given change in effort should have a greater impact on the probability of bankruptcy when the profit share is small or negative to begin with than when it is large. To test this, the variable LIQ, equal to the profit share minus its sample average when the profit share is below the sample average and equal to zero when the profit share exceeds its sample average, was added to the regression. LIQ is thus negative when the profit share falls below its sample mean and zero otherwise. We expect its coefficient to be positive, meaning an additional negative impact on labor hours when the profit share is below its sample mean.

Two lags of LIQ are added to the manufacturing regression using quarterly data. As expected, the sum of the coefficients is positive. The sum is slightly larger than the sum on the profit shares, meaning that a reduction in profits is more than twice as effective at boosting labor productivity growth when profits are already low than when they are high. Unfortunately, multicollinearity of the lagged LIQ with the lagged profit share produce a high standard error, making the result a bit uncertain.

Table 1.17

Test of the Liquidity Constraint Version of the Bankruptcy Hypothesis, by Industry

	Textiles (22)	Paper (26)	Chemicals (28)	Petroleum (29)
AQ\1	106.1	8.6	55.2	9.8
	(119.3)	(33.4)	(48.4)	(9.1)
LIQ\1	81.5	29.8	8.5	-3.9
	(216.9)	(56.7)	(79.5)	(16.4)

	Stone, Clay and Glass (32)	Primary Metals (33)	Fabricated Metals (34)	Nonelectrical Machinery (35)
AQ\1	18.4	27.7	24.5	38.6
	(32.1)	(22.0)	(42.3)	(65.2)
LIQ\1	-12.3	-26.1	15.8	-55.5
	(44.8)	(26.6)	(82.0)	(129.4)

	Electrical Machinery (36)	Motor Vehicles (371)	Other Transportation (372@9)	Manufacturing except SIC 29
AQ\1	85.5	-77.0	65.2	9.8
	(71.4)	(61.9)	(80.8)	(30.2)
LIQ\1	-175.8	72.7	75.9	34.3
	(143.1)	(65.9)	(170.1)	(55.6)

Notes: The dependent variable in each case was %ch(L), the percentage change in the industry's labor hours, defined as the number of employees times weekly hours of production workers. AQ\1 is the lag of the profit share. LIQ\1 is the lag of LIQ, which is described in the text. Also included in the regressions (but not reported here) were a constant, the percentage change in each industry's real GDP, instrumented for by the percentage change in aggregate real GNP, and the lagged percentage change in the industry's labor hours. No coefficients were significant. All regressions were estimated using annual data for 1950-87. Figures in parentheses are standard errors.

In the regression for aggregate manufacturing using annual data, the lag of LIQ again takes a positive, albeit insignificant, coefficient, this time nearly four times as large as that on the profit share (Table 1.17). Oddly, however, the variable has a negative coefficient in 5 of the 11 manufacturing industries tested—petroleum (29), stone, clay and glass (32), primary metals (33), nonelectrical machinery (35), and electrical machinery (36).

Table 1.18

Test of Liquidity Constraint Version of the Bankruptcy Hypothesis by Industry, Using Hours of Full-Time and Part-Time Workers

	Textiles (22)	Paper (26)	Chemicals (28)	Petroleum (29)
AQ\1	85.7	-15.9	117.2*	-8.6
	(131.1)	(25.3)	(47.6)	(5.7)
LIQ\1	84.8	93.6*	-89.1	16.0
	(238.8)	(45.8)	(78.4)	(17.6)

	Stone, Clay and Glass (32)	Primary Metals (33)	Fabricated Metals (34)	Nonelectrical Machinery (35)
AQ\1	-2.0	23.4	-63.4	-9.2
	(25.8)	(22.5)	(61.9)	(42.2)
LIQ\1	31.5	36.0	113.4	65.8
	(66.5)	(70.7)	(121.0)	(75.7)

	Electrical Machinery (36)	Motor Vehicles (371)	Other Transportation (372@9)	Manufacturing except SIC 29
AQ\1	214.4*	-185.5*	-52.3	17.8
	(122.9)	(78.7)	(124.0)	(29.2)
LIQ\1	-404.7	349.6**	271.7	23.4
	(214.3)	(125.3)	(174.7)	(53.5)

Notes: The dependent variable in each case was %ch(L), the percentage change in the industry's labor hours, defined as hours of full-time and part-time workers. AQ\1 is the lag of the profit share. LIQ\1 is the lag of LIQ, which is described in the text. Also included in the regressions (but not reported here) were a constant, the percentage change in each industry's real GDP, instrumented for by the percentage change in aggregate real GNP, and the lagged percentage change in the industry's labor hours. * denotes significance at the 95% level. ** denotes significance at the 99% level. The regression for manufacturing except SIC 29 was estimated using annual data for 1950 to 1987. All other regressions were estimated using annual data for 1950 to 1978. Figures in parentheses are standard errors or SIC codes, where applicable.

The results are quite different when hours of full-time and part-time workers replace the product of employment and weekly hours of production workers as the dependent variable (Table 1.18). At the aggregate level, the coefficient on lagged LIQ is still larger than the coefficient on the lagged profit share, and both coefficients remain insignificant. In this case, however, 9 of the 11 industries have positive LIQ coefficients, two of which are significant—paper (26) and motor vehicles (371). We would, in fact, expect these industries to fit the bankruptcy model particularly well, since they are heavily unionized. In such cases, workers have more to lose from bankruptcy and are more able to coordinate work rule concessions and other productivity enhancements. Thus, this test provides support for the bankruptcy hypothesis.

8. BANKRUPTCY CHOICE MODEL

In the bankruptcy model presented in the last section, workers lose their jobs when the firm can no longer pay its bills. In such cases, cyclical and noncyclical profits will have equivalent effects, since all that matters is total profits. In many cases, such as that of GM's Saturn plant cited earlier, however, bankruptcy of the firm is not really the threat. Instead, workers may fear that their employer will undertake less new investment, or shut down an unprofitable plant. Similar to bankruptcy, this can eliminate existing jobs. In fact, one does see worker concessions similar to those in cases of prospective bankruptcy when a multi-plant firm announces it will modernize some of its existing plants and shut down others, as has happened in the auto industry. To avoid being the plant which is shut down, workers at the various plants may even compete against each other with offers of wage concessions and work rule changes.

In the "bankruptcy by choice" model of this section, the firm declares bankruptcy or shuts down a given plant when the present discounted value (PDV) from continued use of the assets of the firm or plant is less than the value of the assets if sold. In the case of an individual plant, the firm must also consider the effect of the plant's production on the price it receives for goods manufactured at its other plants. Assuming the time horizon over which the PDV is taken is long relative to the duration of cyclical profits, noncyclical profits will play a more substantial role in determining the PDV than cyclical profits will, and thus should have a more significant impact on productivity. This provides a testable difference between the liquidity constraint and bankruptcy by choice models.

While the empirical tests are performed using industry-level data, the bankruptcy by choice model holds at the level of the firm, rather than at the industry level. That is, the firm's profits, not the industry's, determine bankruptcy. In order to make the model applicable at the industry level, we must assume that individual firms are represented by some dispersion around the industry mean. A lower mean is thus assumed to shift the entire distribution of firms' profit levels down. In addition, I assume here that the PDV/resale values of individual plants are distributed around the firm's average.

In the liquidity constraint model of Section 7, bankruptcy is declared if current profits, π, fall below some threshold level W. In the bankruptcy by choice model, the expected PDV of the firm replaces current profits and W becomes the resale value of the firm's capital. Thus, the firm chooses bankruptcy or shuts down a plant in period t if

$$(1.28) \quad W > E(PDV_t) = \sum_{i=0}^{\infty} R^i E(\pi_{t+i}),$$

where the π_{t+i} are profits, R is the discount factor, and E denotes expectations at time t. (All expectations are taken at time t.)

Let

$$(1.29) \quad \pi_{t+i} = \pi^*_{t+i} + D_{t+i} + \mu_{t+i}(X_t, X_{t+1}, \ldots, X_{t+i}),$$

where p^*_{t+i} is what real profits would be in period t+i if, ceteris paribus, demand in period t+i and effort in period t were to take their average levels, D is the cyclical component of profits, normalized to have a zero average, X is effort, and μ relates period t effort to period t+i profits. $\mu' > 0$ and $\mu(X) = 0$ for average X. Expanding equation (1.29), the firm will choose bankruptcy if

$$W > E(PDV_t) = \sum_{i=0}^{\infty} R^i E(\pi^*_{t+i}) + \sum_{i=0}^{\infty} R^i E(D_{t+i})$$

(1.30)

$$+ \sum_{i=0}^{\infty} R^i E(\mu_{t+i}(X_t, X_{t+1}, \ldots, X_{t+i})).$$

I assume that both the cyclical and noncyclical components of profits are autocorrelated, but that the noncyclical component exhibits more persistence. That is, low profits are expected to turn around more quickly if they are caused by a soft economy than if they are caused by other factors. Thus,

(1.31) $D_t = bD_{t-1} + d_t$

and

(1.32) $\pi^*_t = \pi_0 + a(\pi^*_{t-1} - \pi_0) + z_t,$

where $0 < b < a < 1$ and d and z are white noise error terms. D tends toward zero, while π^* tends toward π_0.

X$_t$ is chosen by the workers at the beginning of period t, without knowledge of d$_t$ and z$_t$. The firm makes its period t bankruptcy decision (whether or not to produce in period t) knowing X$_t$, z$_t$, and d$_t$, but without any information about future d and z. We can thus rewrite equation (1.30) as

(1.33)

$$
\begin{aligned}
E(PDV_t) = & \sum_{i=0}^{\infty} R^i \pi_0 + \sum_{i=0}^{\infty} R^i a^{i+1} (\pi^*_{t-1} - \pi_0) + \sum_{i=0}^{\infty} R^i a^i z_t \\
& + \sum_{i=0}^{\infty} R^i b^{i+1} D_{t-1} + \sum_{i=0}^{\infty} R^i b^i d_t \\
& + \sum_{i=0}^{\infty} R^i E(\mu_{t+i} (X_t, X_{t+1}, \ldots, X_{t+i})).
\end{aligned}
$$

Because R is assumed constant,

(1.34)

$$
\begin{aligned}
E(PDV_t) = & \frac{1}{1-R} \pi_0 + \frac{a}{1-aR} (\pi^*_{t-1} - \pi_0) + \frac{1}{1-aR} z_t \\
& + \frac{b}{1-bR} D_{t-1} + \frac{1}{1-bR} d_t + \sum_{i=0}^{\infty} R^i \mu_{t+i} (X_t) \\
& + \sum_{i=0}^{\infty} R^i E(\mu_{t+i} (X_t, X_{t+1}, \ldots, X_{t+i})).
\end{aligned}
$$

The assumption that noncyclical profits are more autocorrelated than cyclical profits means that the noncyclical component has a larger impact on the PDV. Mathematically, this follows because $a/(1-aR)$, the coefficient of π^*_{t-1}, lagged noncyclical profits, is larger than $b/(1-bR)$, the coefficient of D_{t-1}, lagged cyclical profits, when $a > b$.

Although the firm has full information about period t when it makes its bankruptcy decision, workers have no information about period t when they choose X$_t$. Thus, their decision can be modeled using a variant of equation (1.24), the relationship between profits, effort and bankruptcy in the liquidity constraint model:

(1.35) $B = \text{Prob}\left[E(PDV_t) < W\right].$

Substituting from equation (1.34), this implies

$$B = \text{Prob}\left[\frac{1}{1-aR}z_t + \frac{1}{1-bR}d_t < W - \frac{1}{1-R}\pi_0 - \frac{b}{1-bR}D_{t-1}\right.$$

(1.36)
$$\left. - \frac{a}{1-aR}(\pi^*_{t-1} - \pi_0)\right.$$

$$\left. + \sum_{i=0}^{\infty}R^iE\left(\mu_{t+i}(X_t, X_{t+1}, \ldots, X_{t+i})\right)\right].$$

Since workers also have control over future X, the choice of X_t realistically should take into account its impact on future X. The workers' decision becomes analytically intractable in such a case, however, so I assume workers choose X_t myopically. In addition, I assume that workers only look at the impact of X_t on the firm's bankruptcy decision in period t, and not on its decisions in future periods. Once again, this assumption is made for the sake of tractability.

As in the liquidity constraint model, a decline in either cyclical (D_{t-1}) or noncyclical (π^*_{t-1}) profits increases the probability of bankruptcy. Workers can partially offset these lower profits by boosting effort (X), just as in the liquidity constraint model. Because a dollar of noncyclical profits has a larger impact on the bankruptcy decision than a dollar of cyclical profits, however, a given change in the noncyclical component of profits will warrant more of an effort response than an equivalent to change in the cyclical component. This contrasts with the liquidity constraint model, where both components have the same effect, and depends on the assumption that low noncyclical profits are more persistent than low cyclical profits.

The two versions of the bankruptcy hypothesis thus produce different implications concerning the relative effects of cyclical and noncyclical profits. If the simple liquidity constraint hypothesis is correct, cyclical and noncyclical profits will have the same effect on labor productivity, while if the bankruptcy by choice hypothesis is correct, noncyclical profits should be more important. Unfortunately, the U.S. data reviewed in Section 4 do not provide a clear answer.

Table 1.19

Test of Bankruptcy by Choice Hypothesis, Using Stock Prices as a Measure of Present Discounted Value

Constant	-7.2**	-20.3
	(2.3)	(13.2)
%ch(GDP82)	0.81**	0.88**
	(0.04)	(0.06)
%ch(LM\1)	0.04	-0.02
	(0.05)	(0.09)
JS&PIND/K	2.54*	0.00
	(1.47)	(2.04)
AQ\1	38.4*	
	(18.2)	
AQCYC\1		123.2
		(92.6)
AQNONCYC\1		27.5
		(16.7)

Notes: The dependent variable, %ch(LM), is the percent growth in worker hours in manufacturing. %ch(GDP82) is the percentage change in real manufacturing GDP. %ch(LM\1) is %ch(LM), lagged one quarter. JS&PIND is the Standard and Poor's stock price index of 400 industrials. K is the net stock of fixed capital in manufacturing. AQCYC\1 is the lagged cyclical component of AQ. AQNONCYC\1 is the lagged noncyclical component of AQ. AQ\1 is the first lag of the profit share variable described in the text. Real GNP growth was used as an instrument for %ch(GDP82). * denotes significance at the 95% level. ** denotes significance at the 99% level. Both regressions were estimated using annual data for 1950 to 1987. Figures in parentheses are standard errors.

Although noncyclical profits are generally more statistically significant, they also tend to have smaller coefficients. The OECD data (Table 1.16), however, point toward bankruptcy by choice. For each of the four non-U.S. countries tested, noncyclical profits have a higher (or, in the case of Japan, less negative) coefficient than cyclical profits.

A simpler alternative strategy to testing the bankruptcy by choice hypothesis, suggested to me by Eric Rasmusen, is to divide through the bankruptcy condition (1.28) by the bankruptcy threshold W, to get a relative of Tobin's q:[53] "Bankruptcy if

$$(1.37) \quad \frac{PDV}{W} < 1."$$

In this case, W becomes the resale value of the equipment. Assuming, albeit hesitantly, that stock prices are rational, then stockholders' equity should equal the value of "good will" plus the present discounted value of potential future earnings from existing equipment (PDV). We can therefore test the bankruptcy by choice hypothesis by substituting PDV/W for the profit share in the labor hours equation. In the bankruptcy by choice model, condition (1.37) usually applies at the plant level, rather than at the level of the firm. Since any plant's PDV should move with that of its firm, however, any drop in a firm's PDV/W will increase the pressure on some plant, and thus spur productivity growth.

My measure of the present discounted value, PDV, is the Standard and Poor's industrials index. The "resale" value of capital, W, is the BEA's net capital stock measure for manufacturing. The variable PDV/W, thus constructed, is added to the basic labor hours regression of Section 4, in place of profits (Table 1.19). The ratio of present discounted value to resale value is significant at the 95% level. This appears to provide additional support for the bankruptcy hypothesis. In addition, when profits are decomposed into cyclical and noncyclical components, and added back into the equation, the coefficient of PDV/W nearly disappears. This is consistent with the bankruptcy by choice theory if it means that PDV/W is a proxy for noncyclical profits.

9. INDUSTRY CASE STUDY: MOTOR VEHICLES

Company-level data provide another means of testing the bankruptcy hypotheses. In Section 7, we saw that, when hours are measured as hours of full-time and part-time workers, labor productivity growth in the auto industry responds positively to a drop in profits only when profits are already at a low level, i.e., when bankruptcy or plant shutdown is a possibility. Indeed, a heavily unionized industry where workers earn a substantial wage premium satisfies the theoretical conditions for the bankruptcy hypothesis quite well. This section shows that empirical results obtained from regressions for the Big Three auto makers bolster this conclusion and point toward the bankruptcy by choice hypothesis. Low lagged noncyclical profits boost labor productivity growth, while low cyclical profits do not.

Table 1.20
Effect of Profits on Labor Demand: Big Three Automakers

	Big Three	GM	Ford	Chrysler
Constant	-3.7*	-1.5	-3.3*	-3.9
	(1.7)	(3.7)	(1.6)	(4.9)
%ch(output)	0.63**	0.62**	0.49**	0.73**
	(0.10)	(0.17)	(0.10)	(0.22)
AQ\1	1.2	-19.2	-85.7*	16.2
	(30.4)	(105.9)	(40.1)	(56.5)

Notes: The dependent variable is the percentage change in labor hours. %ch(output) is the percentage change in output. AQ\1 is the lagged profit share. All variables are described in the text. * denotes significance at the 95% level. ** denotes significance at the 99% level. All regressions were estimated using annual data for 1980 to 1988. Figures in parentheses are standard errors.

The primary difficulty with running firm-level regressions is finding appropriate data, since neither hours nor real output are directly available. For each Big Three firm, I define hours as the number of employees of the firm, times weekly hours of production workers in the motor vehicle industry (SIC 3711) as a whole. Real output is defined as each company's net sales divided by the producer price index for motor vehicles and equipment. The profit share is defined as net income (income after taxes) before extraordinary items and discontinued operations, divided by nominal net sales.

The percentage change in labor hours was regressed on the percentage change in real output and on the lagged profit share. (The change in lagged hours was deleted both because it had the wrong sign and to add another degree of freedom to a very small sample.) The regression used annual data from 1980 through 1988. When separate equations for each firm are estimated, low lagged profits (relative to the firm's average) have a significant adverse effect on labor productivity growth at Ford, insignificant adverse effects at GM, and insignificant positive effects at Chrysler (Table 1.20). However, when the data are stacked, constraining each variable to have the same coefficient for each company, lagged profits (now relative to the industry average) have a marginally positive effect. The slightly more positive effects of low profits in the full sample imply that low profits relative to those of the industry as a whole produce greater productivity growth than low profits relative to a company's own performance. The

Table 1.21
Effect of Cyclical and Noncyclical Components of Lagged Profits on
Labor Demand: Big Three Automakers

	Big Three	GM	Ford	Chrysler
Constant	-2.1	-3.5	-3.4*	1.6
	(1.7)	(4.4)	(1.7)	(6.4)
%ch(output)	0.56**	0.56*	0.42*	0.56*
	(0.09)	(0.19)	(0.15)	(0.24)
AQCYC\1	-76.1*	11.9	-89.8*	-133.2
	(43.1)	(114.1)	(42.7)	(130.0)
AQNONCYC\1	57.6	104.7	1.5	92.4
	(36.8)	(180.2)	(139.6)	(80.9)

Notes: The dependent variable is the percentage change in labor hours. %ch(output) is the percentage change in output. AQCYC\1 is the lagged cyclical component of the profit share. AQNONCYC\1 is the lagged noncyclical component of the profit share. All variables are described in the text. * denotes significance at the 95% level. ** denotes significance at the 99% level. All regressions were estimated using annual data for 1980 to 1988. Figures in parentheses are standard errors.

disappointing results for aggregate profits are similar to those found above at the industry level.

Dividing profits into its cyclical and noncyclical components provides support for the bankruptcy by choice hypothesis. To accomplish this division, the profit share was regressed on capacity utilization for SIC 371, with the coefficients on the constant and capacity utilization constrained to be equal for each company. Fitted values from the regression are interpreted as cyclical profits, while the residuals form the noncyclical component of profits. These two variables were substituted for the total profit share in the stacked regression. Table 1.21 shows that a high lagged noncyclical profit share reduces productivity growth at the 90% level of significance, while the lagged cyclical profit share does not even have the right sign. As in the case where profits are not divided into cyclical and noncyclical components, however, the noncyclical portion of profits is never significant when separate equations are estimated for each firm, although the coefficient always has the correct sign.

The results from the stacked regression indicate that the recovery of productivity growth at Ford and Chrysler during the 1980s stemmed in large part from these companies' brushes with bankruptcy during the early 1980s. The turnaround was not caused by low cyclical profits, which everyone knew would recover, but from a sharp drop in the component of profits which could not be attributed to weak demand—noncyclical profits. In constrast, productivity growth at GM, where profits did not suffer as badly in the early 1980s, lagged.

10. SUMMARY AND CONCLUSION

The first two sections of this chapter showed that productivity growth responds inversely to profitability, after controlling for normal effects of the business cycle. Two possible explanations for this phenomenon were proposed. In the first of these, managers have a limited amount of time that they can devote toward cost-cutting or sales-increasing activities. When profits per sale are low, they shift time towards cost-cutting, thereby boosting productivity. In the second set of models, workers and managers are more willing to search for and/or adopt more efficient practices when the survival of their firm or plant is at stake. Empirical evidence seems to point towards the latter explanation.

Such an inverse relationship between profits and productivity would explain the behavior of productivity during the late 1980s and early 1990s fairly well. Strong accounting profits during 1987-88, partly due to tax reform's removal of accelerated depreciation, may have led to complacency at many companies, leading to a slowdown in productivity growth. As profits plummeted in 1990-91, however, workers and managers realized that corporate survival depended on productivity gains, resulting in the surge in productivity growth in 1992. The decline in productivity in the first half of 1993 may indicate that improved profits in 1992 have diminished the incentive to raise productivity. If so, the "new era" of faster productivity growth has come to an abrupt end.

Although the results documented in this study can explain productivity behavior during such episodes as the late 1980s and early 1990s, it is difficult to believe that productivity growth has slowed in the past two decades due to too-high profits. Given the lack of success of traditional explanations for the productivity slowdown, however, this study does imply that behavioral theories may be a useful avenue down which to pursue a satisfactory explanation for the productivity slowdown.

Before drawing policy conclusions from the results of this study, it is important to note that I have focused on only one part of the relationship between profits and productivity. Profits, or at least the profit motive, also has a significant positive influence on productivity. One has only to look at the abysmal productivity performance of the command economies over the last few decades to see that the profit motive is crucial to improving living standards. To use the results of this study to argue that anything which reduces profits must be good for productivity is to throw the baby out with the bath water.

One potential policy implication is important enough to mention, however: protectionism probably inhibits productivity growth. This study implies that the threat of lost jobs from foreign competition can be a powerful stimulus to the adoption of more efficient, less costly methods of production. In fact, pressure for protectionism is likely to be strongest where workers have the most to lose—exactly the situation where the bankruptcy theory indicates workers will be willing to make the greatest sacrifices to save their jobs. As the old saying puts it, "Necessity is the mother of invention."

APPENDIX A. DERIVATION OF EQUATION 1.4

To derive equation (1.4), begin with equation (1.3):

(1.3)
$$L_t = \frac{b}{b+bR+c}L_{t-1} + \frac{bR}{b+bR+c}E_t L_{t+1} + \frac{c}{b+bR+c}L^*_t$$
$$+ \frac{c}{b+bR+c}X_t - \frac{c}{b+bR+c}X'.$$

Rewrite this, using the backshift operator, B, as:

(1A.1)
$$\frac{c}{b+bR+c}L^*_t + \frac{c}{b+bR+c}X_t - \frac{c}{b+bR+c}X' =$$
$$= L_t - \frac{b}{b+bR+c}BL_t - \frac{bR}{b+bR+c}B^{-1}L_t$$
$$= -\frac{b}{b+bR+c}BL_t\left(1 - \frac{b+bR+c}{b}B^{-1} + RB^{-2}\right).$$

Now define f and g so that

(1A.2)
$$\frac{c}{b+bR+c}L^*_t + \frac{c}{b+bR+c}X_t - \frac{c}{b+bR+c}X' =$$
$$= -\frac{b}{b+bR+c}BL_t\left(1 - fB^{-1}\right)\left(1 - gB^{-1}\right)$$
$$= -\frac{b}{b+bR+c}\left(BL_t - fL_t\right)\left(1 - gB^{-1}\right)$$
$$= \frac{b}{b+bR+c}\left(L_t - \frac{1}{f}L_{t-1}\right)\left(1 - gB^{-1}\right).$$

Multiplying through by (b+bR+c)/bf produces

(1A.3)
$$\frac{c}{bf}L^*_t + \frac{c}{bf}X_t - \frac{c}{bf}X' = \left(L_t - \frac{1}{f}L_{t-1}\right)\left(1 - gB^{-1}\right).$$

Applying the quadratic formula to equation (1A.2), we know that

(1A.4)
$$f + g = \frac{b+bR+c}{b} = 1 + R + \frac{c}{b}$$

and

(1A.5)
$$fg = R.$$

Because $1+R+(c/b)$ is greater than one, and R is greater than zero, f and g must both be positive. Combining equations (1A.4) and (1A.5), we also find that

(1A.6) $\quad f + g - fg - 1 = c/b > 0.$

Factoring the left-hand side of (1A.6) and multiplying through by -1 yields:

(1A.7) $\quad (f-1)(g-1) < 0.$

Since f and g are both positive, one of the two (say f) must be greater than one, while the other (g) is less than one.

Since g is less than 1, we can divide equation (1A.3) through by $(1-gB^{-1})$, and convert the two $1/(1-gB^{-1})$ into infinite series:

(1A.8)
$$\frac{c}{bf}\sum_{i=0}^{\infty}g^i E_t L^*_{t+i} + \frac{c}{bf}\sum_{i=0}^{\infty}g^i E_t X_{t+i}$$
$$-\frac{c}{bf}\sum_{i=0}^{\infty}g^i X' = L_t - \frac{1}{f}L_{t-1},$$

where E_t denotes expectations at time t. This can be rewritten as

(1A.9)
$$\frac{c}{bf}\frac{1}{1-g}L^*_t + \frac{c}{bf}\sum_{i=1}^{\infty}g^i(E_t L^*_{t+i} - L^*_t)$$
$$+\frac{c}{bf}\frac{1}{1-g}X_t + \frac{c}{bf}\sum_{i=1}^{\infty}g^i(E_t X_{t+i} - X_t)$$
$$-\frac{c}{bf}\frac{1}{1-g}X' = L_t - \frac{1}{f}L_{t-1}.$$

Since $c/b = (f-1)(1-g)$, (1A.9) can be rewritten as

(1A.10)
$$\left(1-\frac{1}{f}\right)L^*_t + \left(1-\frac{1}{f}\right)(1-g)\sum_{i=1}^{\infty}g^i(E_t L^*_{t+i} - L^*_t)$$
$$+\left(1-\frac{1}{f}\right)(X_t - X')$$
$$+\left(1-\frac{1}{f}\right)(1-g)\sum_{i=1}^{\infty}g^i(E_t X_{t+i} - X_t) = L_t - \frac{1}{f}L_{t-1}.$$

If effort is not autocorrelated, then $E_t X_{t+i} = X'$ for all $i > 1$. In this case,

$$(1A.11) \quad \left(1 - \frac{1}{f}\right)(1-g)\sum_{i=1}^{\infty} g^i \left(E_t X_{t+i} - X_t\right) = \left(1 - \frac{1}{f}\right)g(X' - X_t).$$

Suppose instead that there is some positive autocorrelation of effort, at least in the short run. Assuming that $E_t X_{t+i} - X_t$ equals $X' - X_t$ times a factor F_i, which lies between zero and one, then (1A.10) can be rewritten as

$$(1A.12) \quad \left(1 - \frac{1}{f}\right)L^*_t + \left(1 - \frac{1}{f}\right)(1-g)\sum_{i=1}^{\infty} g^i \left(E_t L^*_{t+i} - L^*_t\right)$$
$$+ \beta_3(X_t - X') = L_t - \frac{1}{f}L_{t-1},$$

where $(1-1/f) \geq \beta_3 \geq (1-1/f)(1-g)$. ($\beta_3$ equals $1-1/f$ when all the F_i equal zero, and equals $(1-1/f)(1-g)$ when all the F_i equal one.) Replacing $1/f$ with β_1, g with β_2, and rearranging terms, equation (1A.12) becomes

$$(1.4) \quad L_t = \beta_1 L_{t-1} + (1-\beta_1)L^*_t + \beta_3(X_t - X')$$
$$+ (1-\beta_1)(1-\beta_2)\sum_{i=1}^{\infty} \beta_2^i (E_t L^*_{t+i} - L^*_t).$$

It can be shown by solving for f that as c/b increases--as the relative importance of adjustment costs decline--β_1 decreases.

APPENDIX B. EFFECT OF HIGHER PROFITS ON TIME ALLOCATED TO COST-CUTTING

In this appendix, I show that an increase in the period 1 profit share causes managers to devote less time to cost-cutting activities in period 2. We begin with the firm's maximization problem as specified in the text. Recall that $\partial S_2/\partial s_2$, $\partial S_2/\partial S_1$, $\partial P_2/\partial p_2$ and $\partial P_2/\partial P_1$ are all positive. Also, $\partial^2 S_2/\partial s_2^2 < 0$ and $\partial^2 P_2/\partial p_2^2 < 0$. For simplicity's sake, $\partial^2 P_2/(\partial p_2 \partial P_1)$ is assumed equal to zero. Also, $s_2 + p_2 = T$, so that $ds_2 = -dp_2$. Rewriting equation (18) in differential form:

(1B.1)
$$\frac{\partial^2 S_2}{\partial s_2^2} ds_2 P_2 + \frac{\partial S_2}{\partial s_2}\left(\frac{\partial P_2}{\partial p_2} dp_2 + \frac{\partial P_2}{\partial P_1} dP_1\right) =$$
$$\frac{\partial^2 P_2}{\partial p_2^2} dp_2 S_2 + \frac{\partial^2 P_2}{\partial p_2 \partial P_1} dP_1 S_2 + \frac{\partial P_2}{\partial p_2}\frac{\partial S_2}{\partial s_2} ds_2 .$$

Set $\partial^2 P_2/(\partial p_2 \partial P_1) = 0$ and $ds_2 = -dp_2$. Divide through the result by dP_1 to get:

(1B.2)
$$-\frac{\partial^2 S_2}{\partial s_2^2}\frac{dp_2}{dP_1} P_2 + \frac{\partial S_2}{\partial s_2}\frac{\partial P_2}{\partial p_2}\frac{dp_2}{dP_1} + \frac{\partial S_2}{\partial s_2}\frac{\partial P_2}{\partial P_1} =$$
$$\frac{\partial^2 P_2}{\partial p_2^2}\frac{dp_2}{dP_1} S_2 - \frac{\partial P_2}{\partial p_2}\frac{\partial S_2}{\partial s_2}\frac{dp_2}{dP_1} .$$

Grouping together the dp_2/dP_1 terms and rearranging produces

(1B.3)
$$\frac{dp_2}{dP_1} = \frac{\dfrac{\partial S_2}{\partial s_2}\dfrac{\partial P_2}{\partial P_1}}{\dfrac{\partial^2 S_2}{\partial s_2^2} P_2 - 2\dfrac{\partial S_2}{\partial s_2}\dfrac{\partial P_2}{\partial p_2} + \dfrac{\partial^2 P_2}{\partial p_2^2} S_2} .$$

We want to show that dp_2/dP_1 is negative. The numerator is the impact of an increase in current profits per sale on the marginal value of non-price competition time (the residual of cost-cutting time). Non-price competition time becomes more valuable, so this is positive. The denominator is the impact of an increase in cost-cutting time (and a corresponding decrease in non-price competition time) on the marginal value of cost-cutting time. Decreasing returns means this is negative. The entire expression, dp_2/dP_1, is thus negative, meaning that an increase in past profits per sale reduces the amount of time spent in cutting costs, thus reducing the observed current level of productivity.

APPENDIX C. EFFECT OF PROFITS ON MANAGER RETENTION

This appendix shows that an increase in the lagged profit share (P_1), in the model of Section 6, causes $d\pi_2/dA$ to increase. To solve for the effect of a change in P_1 on $d\pi_2/dA$, simply take the derivative of $d\pi_2/dA$ with respect to P_1:

(1C.1)
$$\frac{d^2\pi_2}{dA\,dP_1} = s_2\,\frac{\partial S_2}{\partial(A s_2)}\,\frac{\partial P_2}{\partial P_1} + \frac{ds_2}{dP_1}\,\frac{\partial S_2}{\partial(A s_2)}\,P_2 - \frac{S_2 p_2}{A^2}\,\frac{\partial^2 P_2}{\partial p_2\,\partial P_1}$$
$$-\frac{S_2}{A^2}\,\frac{\partial P_2}{\partial p_2}\,\frac{\partial p_2}{\partial P_1} + 2\,\frac{S_2 p_2}{A^3}\,\frac{\partial P_2}{\partial p_2}\,\frac{dA}{dP_1}.$$

Because $\partial^2 P_2/(\partial p_2 \partial P_1) = 0$ and $dA/dP_1 = 0$ by assumption (a manager cannot change his or her characteristics):

(1C.2)
$$\frac{d^2\pi_2}{dA\,dP_1} = s_2\,\frac{\partial S_2}{\partial(A s_2)}\,\frac{\partial P_2}{\partial P_1} + \frac{ds_2}{dP_1}\,\frac{\partial S_2}{\partial(A s_2)}\,P_2 - \frac{S_2}{A^2}\,\frac{\partial P_2}{\partial p_2}\,\frac{\partial p_2}{\partial P_1}.$$

Solving the firm's maximization problem, we find that the new first order conditions for allocation of time between s and p yield the equation

(1C.3)
$$A\,\frac{\partial S_2}{\partial(A s_2)}\,P_2 = \frac{\partial P_2}{\partial p_2}\,\frac{S_2}{A}.$$

Dividing through by A and multiplying by $ds_2/dP_1 = -dp_2/dP_1$,

(1C.4)
$$\frac{ds_2}{dP_1}\,\frac{\partial S_2}{\partial(A s_2)}\,P_2 = -\frac{S_2}{A^2}\,\frac{\partial P_2}{\partial p_2}\,\frac{dp_2}{dP_1}.$$

This allows us to combine terms in equation (1C.2) to get:

(1C.5)
$$\frac{d^2\pi_2}{dA\,dP_1} = s_2\,\frac{\partial S_2}{\partial(A s_2)}\,\frac{\partial P_2}{\partial P_1} + 2\,\frac{ds_2}{dP_1}\,\frac{\partial S_2}{\partial(A s_2)}\,P_2.$$

Since ds_2/dP_1 is positive as in the previous model, this expression is unambiguously positive.

APPENDIX D. EFFECT OF PROFITS ON EFFORT

In this appendix, I want to show mathematically that, in the model of Section 7, an increase in π_1, the base level of profits, reduces current effort. To show this, I must first convert equation (1.26) to a differential, then solve for $dX/d\pi_1$, and then show that $dX/d\pi_1$ (the effect of a change in profits on effort) is negative.

First, rewrite equation (1.26) in differential form:

(1D.1) $\dfrac{\partial U}{\partial Y}\dfrac{\partial Y}{\partial B}\left(\dfrac{\partial^2 B}{\partial X \partial \pi_1}d\pi_1 + \dfrac{\partial^2 B}{\partial X^2}dX\right) + \dfrac{\partial^2 U}{\partial X^2}dX = 0.$

(For the purpose of simplifying second derivatives, it is assumed that $\partial^2 U/(\partial Y \partial X) = 0$, i.e., the level of income does not affect the disutility of an extra unit of effort.) Now we divide through by $d\pi_1$:

(1D.2) $\dfrac{\partial U}{\partial Y}\dfrac{\partial Y}{\partial B}\left(\dfrac{\partial^2 B}{\partial X \partial \pi_1} + \dfrac{\partial^2 B}{\partial X^2}\dfrac{dX}{d\pi_1}\right) + \dfrac{\partial^2 U}{\partial X^2}\dfrac{dX}{d\pi_1} = 0.$

Rearranging (1D.2) yields

(1D.3) $\dfrac{dX}{d\pi_1} = \dfrac{-\left(\dfrac{\partial U}{\partial Y}\dfrac{\partial Y}{\partial B}\right)\dfrac{\partial^2 B}{\partial X \partial \pi_1}}{\left(\dfrac{\partial U}{\partial Y}\dfrac{\partial Y}{\partial B}\right)\dfrac{\partial^2 B}{\partial X^2} + \dfrac{\partial^2 U}{\partial X^2}}.$

All that remains is to show that $dX/d\pi_1$ is negative.

In order to do this, we must determine the signs for $\partial^2 B/(\partial X \partial \pi_1)$ and $\partial^2 B/\partial X^2$. Since $\partial B/\partial \pi_1 = b\partial B/\partial X$, the signs for the two expressions are equivalent. Assume that e is described by a probability density function with only one local maximum (i.e., one hump). Also, assume that e is smaller than its value at this maximum, i.e., to the right of the maximum in Chart 1.4. The derivative of B (probability of bankruptcy) with respect to X depends on where the firm is in the tail of this distribution. The higher is π_1, the farther the firm moves to the right. An increase in effort is less effective at reducing the bankruptcy rate, so $\partial B/\partial X$ becomes less negative. Since high π_1 increases $\partial B/\partial X$, $\partial^2 B/(\partial X \partial \pi_1)$ is positive. Because $\partial^2 B/(\partial X \partial \pi_1) = b\partial^2 B/\partial X^2$, $\partial^2 B/\partial X^2$ is also positive.

We can now determine the sign of the expression in equation (1D.3). $\partial U/\partial Y > 0$ and $\partial Y/\partial B < 1$, so $(\partial U/\partial Y)(\partial Y/\partial B)(\partial^2 B/\partial X \partial \pi_1)$ is negative. Intuitively, $(\partial U/\partial Y)(\partial Y/\partial B)(\partial B/\partial X)$ is the marginal impact of effort on utility through the bankruptcy channel. $(\partial U/\partial Y)(\partial Y/\partial B)(\partial^2 B/\partial X \partial \pi_1)$ is thus the change in this impact due to a change in the profit level. As today's profits become larger, an extra unit of effort is less effective at increasing utility, since it has less effect on the bankruptcy rate (the firm is moving farther into the tail of the distribution).

As for the denominator of the expression in equation (1D.3), the first term represents the change in $(\partial U/\partial Y)(\partial Y/\partial B)(\partial B/\partial X)$—the marginal impact of greater effort on utility through the bankruptcy channel—given a higher initial level of effort. Because of decreasing marginal returns to effort, this is negative. The second term is the increasing marginal disutility of effort, which is also negative. Thus, the denominator shows that as the level of effort increases, an extra unit is more costly in terms of utility and less helpful in terms of avoiding bankruptcy. The latter is true because extra effort moves us farther into the tail. Since both numerator and denominator are negative, the minus sign in the numerator makes the whole expression, $dX/d\pi_1$, negative.

                                                                    Q.E.D.

NOTES

1. Perry and Schultze, 1993.
2. Gordon, 1993, 273-74.
3. Denison, 1979.
4. Norsworthy, Harper, and Kunze, 1979.
5. Weisskopf, Bowles, and Gordon, 1983.
6. Nelson, 1981.
7. Sachs, 1983.
8. Smith, 1937, 578.
9. To obtain this concept, the logarithm of productivity was regressed on a constant, a time trend with a kink in 1973, and the change in the logarithm of GDP divided by potential GDP. The final term times its coefficient was then subtracted from the logarithm of productivity. Cyclically-adjusted productivity was then calculated as the exponential of the resulting expression.
10. Sims, 1974; Clark, 1984.
11. For example, Nordhaus, 1972.
12. For example, Sims, 1974.
13. Fair, 1968.
14. Also included in Clark's regression was a term equal to the ratio of actual GNP to potential GNP, meant to capture the effect of high output on the composition of output. That is, cyclically sensitive industries have higher levels of labor productivity. As output increases, labor productivity will thus rise (i.e., labor hours fall, ceteris paribus) simply because of aggregation effects.
15. A Dickey-Fuller test shows that in addition to the random walk term, there is a negative autocorrelation among the errors in this equation. Such errors might result from transitory disturbances in the labor hours equation. In the first difference labor hours equation, this error is subsumed in e.
16. Pagano and Hartley, 1975.
17. Amemiya, 1985.
18. For example, Denison, 1979.
19. Griliches, 1980.
20. Nordhaus, 1972.
21. The DRI/McGraw-Hill measure of potential GNP was used, extrapolated backward from 1957:2, the earliest date for which data were available.
22. Gordon, 1979, 1993.
23. Gordon, 1979.
24. Gordon, 1993.
25. Dickens, 1982.
26. Allen and Link, 1984.
27. For example, Akerlof, 1984; Shapiro and Stiglitz, 1984; Yellen, 1984.

28. Sachs, 1983.

29. These data are unavailable prior to 1955. However, a fairly stable relationship between the total unemployment rate and the rate for married men prevailed during the period 1955-58. I thus assume that the unemployment rate for married men during 1950-54 equalled the civilian unemployment rate minus 1.6 percentage points (the average difference between the two rates during 1955-58).

30. For example, Sachs, 1983.

31. Blanchard and Diamond, 1990.

32. Davis and Haltiwanger, 1990.

33. Clark, 1984.

34. Feldstein and Summers, 1977.

35. Simon, 1959.

36. Cyert and March, 1963.

37. Leibenstein, 1976, 93, 125, 130, 162.

38. Williamson, 1963, 241-42.

39. Williamson, 1963, 241-46.

40. Williamson, 1964, 94-98.

41. Williamson, 1964, 99-119.

42. Williamson, 1963, 242.

43. Williamson, 1964, 111, 121.

44. Kilby, 1962.

45. Williamson, 1964, 122.

46. Hall, 1991.

47. Gary Cohn, "Eastern Airlines Is Expected to Seek New Wage Concessions as Profit Nears," *Wall Street Journal*, 28 Sept. 1984.

48. Dale D. Buss and Doron P. Levin, "GM Is Facing Hard Job As It Revs Up to Change its Business Ways at Saturn," *Wall Street Journal*, 10 Jan. 1985.

49. Weisskopf, Bowles, and Gordon, 1983.

50. Hamermesh, 1986.

51. Leibenstein, 1976, 98-99.

52. As long as the profit share is a monotonically increasing function of the level of profits, then for every V which satisfies the condition "bankruptcy if $\pi < V$," where π is the level of profits, we can find some W which makes the condition "bankruptcy if $\pi_2 < W$," where π_2 is the profit share, equivalent.

For example, let the profit level be determined by the relationship

$$\pi = AQ - B,$$

where Q is output, and A and B are parameters. As long as A and B are positive, then both the profit share and profit level are procyclical, consistent with the actual behavior of profits. The condition "bankruptcy if $\pi > V$" is then equivalent to the condition "bankruptcy if $Q < (B+V)/A$." If we define

$W = A - AB/(B+V)$, this bankruptcy condition is in turn equivalent to the condition "bankruptcy if $Q < B/(A-W)$." Solving this expression for W yields the condition "bankruptcy if $\pi_2 < W$," which is thus equivalent to "bankruptcy if $\pi < V$." Not only does the former bankruptcy condition fit the bankruptcy model better, but it makes more intuitive sense, since V should vary with firm size, while W should not.

53. In Tobin's q theory, investment depends on PDV/W. See Tobin, 1969.

II.

Deferred Marginal Cost: An Explanation for High Estimated Markups

1. INTRODUCTION

Marginal cost is the cost of the additional inputs, such as labor and capital, required to produce an additional unit of good or service. If the question is how to measure this concept empirically using time series data, an intuitive answer would be to divide each period's change in output by that period's change in inputs, adjusting for the effects of exogenous productivity growth. I argue in this chapter that such a calculation gives misleading results, because it ignores the role of labor effort, which businesses can use to postpone marginal cost. Businesses desire to postpone marginal cost in order to reduce the adjustment costs associated with changing the number of workers.

Assuming "effective" labor hours are the true labor input into production, then "effort" is defined as effective hours divided by actual hours. Effort thus makes up for differences between actual labor hours and the labor input into production. For example, when output, and thus the need for effective hours, increases, firms increase actual labor hours less than proportionately, because of the costs of hiring more workers and the costs of increasing hours per worker (overtime). (This phenomenon—short run increasing returns to labor—has long been a robust empirical finding, standing up across industries and across OECD countries.)[1] The gap between the increase in effective hours and the smaller increase in actual hours are made up by an increase in effort. Similarly, when output falls, actual hours fall by less than effective hours, as businesses seek to avoid the loss of trained workers and lower employee morale that a larger cut in hours might produce. The rising gap between actual and effective hours results in reduced effort.

Eventually, changes in effective hours are fully matched by changes in actual hours, pushing effort back to its original level. I call the portion of the adjustment in actual hours which occurs after the initial change in output "deferred marginal cost."

John Shea has found empirical evidence for procyclical variations in effort. After controlling for several factors, including average weekly hours, average overtime hours, the number of recent hires, the percentage of nonproduction workers in the workforce and new investment (corresponding to new and unfamiliar machinery), Shea finds that accident rates per paid hour varied positively with the cycle during the 1973-81 period. Assuming that accidents only occur while workers are working, rather than when they are idle, this means that effort (in this case, the amount of work per paid hour) varies with output. Shea also finds that, for both supermarkets and pharmacies, tasks performed per worker per unit of time depend significantly on output.[2]

Like any other input to production, effort must have some cost—otherwise, an infinite amount would be used. One possibility, examined in this chapter, is that the cost of using effort results from an "implicit" contract in which workers exert greater-than-normal effort now in return for being able to exert less-than-normal effort later. In the case of a downturn, workers pay the firm back for reduced effort now with above-normal effort in later periods. Alternatively, the firm could compensate the workers for fluctuations in effort by changing the wage, but liquidity-constrained workers will prefer fluctuations in effort to fluctuations in the wage.

Chart 2.1 shows the response of actual hours to a permanent increase in output under such an implicit contract. (The contract also applies to temporary shocks, although they are not discussed here because they are more complicated.) At time T_1, output increases, pushing effective hours from H_0 to H_2. The firm's initial response is to boost actual hours to H_1, making up the difference between effective and actual hours with above-normal effort. At time T_1, the firm has adjusted employee hours to the new long run level. However, it has also accumulated an "effort debt"—above-normal effort it must pay

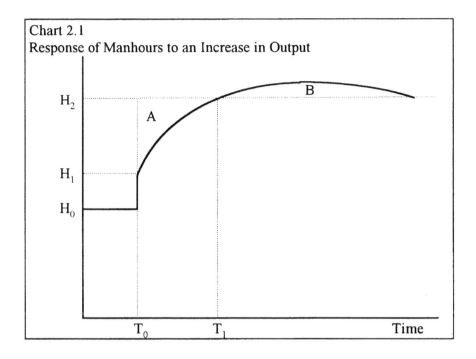

Chart 2.1
Response of Manhours to an Increase in Output

back to its workers in the future in the form of below-normal effort—equal to area A. The firm pays effort back by holding actual hours above effective hours (by overhiring) for a period of time. The area of B, which represents the repayment of effort, will roughly equal the area of A.

The existence of deferred marginal cost has some important economic implications. First, marginal cost measures based on change in output divided by change in inputs will give incorrect readings if deferred marginal cost is not accounted for. In a recent series of papers, Robert Hall has used just such a measure of marginal cost to argue that the ratio of price to marginal cost in U.S. industry is surprisingly high, and thus that U.S. companies have much more market power than previously thought.[3] In this chapter, I will show that adjusting for deferred marginal cost sharply reduces the measured ratio of price to marginal cost.

Second, failing to account for deferred marginal cost distorts the behavior of productivity over the business cycle. Real business cycle theory uses the positive correlation between output growth and productivity growth to argue that fluctuations in productivity growth cause the business cycle. Periods of high productivity are viewed as encouraging greater utilization of labor and capital. If the high productivity results simply from incomplete adjustment of actual to effective labor hours, however, then causality runs from rapid output growth to rapid productivity growth, and not the other way around.

Section 2 of this chapter modifies Hall's estimation procedure to allow for deferred marginal cost, and concludes that Hall introduced a significant upward bias to estimates of the markup of price over marginal cost by failing to account for it. Further evidence for deferred marginal cost is provided by the fact that Hall's estimation procedure produces significantly larger markups at quarterly than at annual frequencies. That is, if marginal cost is deferred as in Chart 2.1, then more marginal cost is deferred beyond the current quarter than beyond the current year. Most of the discrepancy between quarterly and annual markups is eliminated when deferred marginal cost is accounted for.

Even after adjusting for deferred marginal cost, however, a significant difference between the estimated markup and the average markup (value added divided by labor and capital costs) remains. The third section of the chapter attempts to explain this by relaxing the constraint imposed in Section 2 that increased labor hours are the only cost of boosting output. The marginal benefit of capital (labor compensation saved per dollar of capital rented), which Hall estimated to be negative, is shown to be between zero and one once we account for deferred marginal labor cost. Even so, the markup is still significantly higher than the ratio of value added to costs. Firms behave as if boosting output involves deferred capital costs as well as deferred labor costs.

The rest of the chapter discusses the implicit contract by which marginal costs are deferred. Section 4 lays out the evidence for such a contract, and addresses Hall's criticisms that such a contract cannot explain his results. In addition, I discuss the reasons firms would want such a contract, and why variations in effort are repaid with offsetting variations in effort, rather than with variations in the wage rate.

Section 5 discusses an example of such an implicit contract. I show that the contract leaves both utility-maximizing workers and a profit-maximizing firm at least as well off as a constant-effort contract. Variations in real output are shown to generate procyclical variations in productivity. Assuming ex post fixed proportions, labor demand as a function of output and past and future expected hours takes the traditional form, but also contains a term reflecting the "effort debt" of the firm to its workers. The resulting cyclical path followed by labor hours is shown to closely parallel Robert Gordon's "end-of-expansion" phenomenon, in which labor productivity increases less (declines more) than expected after cyclical peaks in real output and rises more (declines less) than expected after cyclical troughs.

Section 6 considers an alternative form for the implicit contract, in which the firm must compensate workers for high effort immediately, possibly with higher wages. Such a contract would be possible in cases where workers cannot be expected to remain with a firm long enough to be compensated for fluctuations in effort now with offsetting variations at a later date. The firm finds it advantageous to let effort vary (and thus reduce variations in labor hours) both because costs of adjusting labor are reduced and because workers will accept a lower wage to reduce the probability of layoff. Section 7 offers concluding remarks.

2. EVIDENCE FOR DEFERRED MARGINAL COST

Robert Hall, using a definition of marginal cost which ignores deferred marginal cost, has found estimates for price divided by marginal cost (both excluding materials) of 1.61 for nondurable manufacturing and 1.62 for durable manufacturing. Even after accounting for variations in the capital stock, the markup is 1.67 for total manufacturing. He also estimated that several industries, including chemicals, paper, motor vehicles and primary metals, have price-cost ratios exceeding 2.0.[4]

A natural question to ask is why profits are on average less than 20% of value added if the markup ratio is greater than 1.6? Hall's answer is that, in order to produce any output at all, firms must invest in capital up to some minimum efficient scale. Initial entrants to an industry produce to capacity and earn positive profits. As other firms with differentiated products enter the industry, however, existing firms find it optimal to produce at less than capacity. Prices fall and profits are bid away so that, in a mature industry, all firms operate with chronic excess capacity. Not only do firms operate with excess capacity, but maintaining this extra capital diverts labor and thus actually reduces output—Hall claimed that the shadow value of capital, at the margin, is negative. (He defined the shadow value of capital as capital's value in minimizing costs—a negative value meaning that additional capital makes production more costly.) New entrants as well as established firms continue to maintain excess capacity, however, because they must maintain minimum efficient scale to produce at all.[5] Hall's definition of marginal cost thus leads him to the paradox that minimum efficient scale coexists with a negative shadow value of capital.

Perhaps the most perplexing feature of Hall's work is that the familiar explanations of short run increasing returns to labor ("SRIRL") fail to explain why the ratio of price to marginal cost should be so high. The most widely accepted of these explanations is labor hoarding. Because of the adjustment costs of changing the number of workers, a firm prefers to keep its workers on during a slump and prefers to put off hiring new workers in an upturn. Since the change in output is less than proportional to the change in labor hours, we observe short run increasing returns to labor (assuming that capital utilization does not fluctuate substantially more than output).

Hall, however, correctly pointed out that this means only that marginal cost is much lower than average cost. If a firm is hoarding labor, then its marginal cost of increasing production is almost nothing.[6] The question becomes: Why don't firms utilize this hoarded labor, given that the cost of doing so is minimal? Hall's answer would be that the firm must fear that prices will fall as a result, because it has substantial market power.

This section provides empirical evidence that part of the marginal cost the firm must pay for increased output is not borne during the current period. This biases Hall's estimates of marginal cost downward, and thus his estimates of the markup, μ, upward. Similarly, when output falls, part of the reduction in costs does not occur during the current period. Thus, the marginal cost, i.e., the reduction in costs for a drop in output, is biased downward.

Hall assumed that the marginal cost of an extra unit of production, x, is $w\Delta N/(\Delta Q - \theta Q)$—where w is the wage, N is labor hours, Q is output, and θ is the rate of labor-augmenting technical progress.[7] (This equation and the following analysis also apply to reductions in cost associated with reduced output. In such cases, both ΔN and $\Delta Q - \theta Q$ are negative.)

In this study, I assume instead that the marginal cost of an extra unit of production may be distributed over time, so that

$$(2.1) \qquad x_t = \sum_{i=1}^{T} \frac{R^i w_{t+i} \Delta N_{t+i,t}}{\Delta Q_t - \theta Q_t} ,$$

where R is the discount factor and $\Delta N_{t+i,t}$ denotes the change in labor hours occurring between periods $t+i-1$ and $t+i$ due to increased production in period t. For all $i > 0$, such changes are deferred marginal cost. To simplify the analysis, assume $\Delta N_{t+1,t} = 0$ for $i > 1$. The labor hours function derived in Section 5 allows for both the possibilities of a longer-lasting series of increases in N and of increases in N prior to anticipated changes in output.

In contrast to Hall's work, where marginal cost and the wage could be real or nominal, equation (2.1) makes no sense unless w is the real wage, meaning x must be the real marginal cost. I assume that the real wage is unaffected by output, and thus that equation (2.1) captures all aspects of marginal cost. Also, I use the approximation $w_{t+i} = R w_{t+i+1}$, i.e., $w_t = R w_{t+1}$. The errors this may introduce into the estimate of x—possibly as large as 5% in some years—are still small in a discussion of why markups are 50% larger than expected.

Substituting this approximation for future real wages into equation (2.1) produces

$$(2.2) \qquad x_t = \frac{w_t \Delta N_{t,t} + w_t \Delta N_{t+1,t}}{\Delta Q_t - \theta Q_t} .$$

Now suppose that marginal cost is distributed over time in such a way that

$$(2.3) \qquad \Delta N_{t+1,t} = a \Delta N_{t,t} ,$$

i.e., a fraction $a/(1+a)$ of the change in hours caused by a change in output in period t is deferred to period $t+1$. Then, substituting (2.3) into (2.2) produces another expression for marginal cost,

$$(2.4) \qquad x_t = \frac{w_t(1+a)\Delta N_{t,t}}{\Delta Q_t - \theta Q_t}$$

or

$$(2.5) \qquad x_t(\Delta Q_t - \theta Q_t) = w_t(1+a)\Delta N_{t,t} .$$

Now lag equation (2.5) by one period, multiply through by a/R, use the approximations $w_t = w_{t-1}/R$ and $x_t = x_{t-1}/R$ and add the result to (2.5):

(2.6)
$$x_t(\Delta Q_t - \theta Q_t) + ax_t(\Delta Q_{t-1} - \theta Q_{t-1}) =$$
$$w_t(1+a)(\Delta N_{t,t} + a\Delta N_{t-1,t-1}).$$

Equation (2.3) tells us that the current change in labor hours is the sum of changes due to this period's shock and last period's shock:

(2.7) $\Delta N_t = \Delta N_{t,t} + \Delta N_{t,t-1} = \Delta N_{t,t} + a\Delta N_{t-1,t-1}$.

This can be substituted directly into the right hand side of equation (2.6) to obtain:

(2.8) $x_t(\Delta Q_t - \theta Q_t) + ax_t(\Delta Q_{t-1} - \theta Q_{t-1}) = w_t(1+a)\Delta N_t$.

In the same way as Hall,[8] we can divide through by $x_t Q_t$ and multiply through the right hand side by $p_t Q_t(N_t/p_t Q_t)/N_t$ (where p is the price) to get:

(2.9) $$\dfrac{\Delta Q_t}{Q_t} - \theta + a\dfrac{\Delta Q_{t-1}}{Q_t} - a\theta\dfrac{Q_{t-1}}{Q_t} = \dfrac{p_t}{x_t}\dfrac{w_t N_t}{p_t Q_t}(1+a)\dfrac{\Delta N_t}{N_t}$$.

Although the wage and marginal cost are both real, changing them to nominal values leaves the equation unchanged, since the two appear in numerator and denominator.

Hall assumed p_t/x_t, the markup, is constant over all t, so, following Hall, we will drop those subscripts and relabel the markup as μ. Using the approximation $Q_{t-1}/Q_t = 1$ to convert the final left-hand side term to $-a\theta$, and shifting terms to the right hand side:

(2.10) $$\dfrac{\Delta Q_t}{Q_t} = \mu\dfrac{w_t N_t}{p_t Q_t}(1+a)\dfrac{\Delta N_t}{N_t} - a\dfrac{\Delta Q_{t-1}}{Q_{t-1}} + (1+a)\theta$$.

This is similar to Hall's equation

(2.11) $$\dfrac{\Delta Q}{Q} = \mu\dfrac{wN}{pQ}\dfrac{\Delta N}{N} + \theta + u$$,

where u is the error term in the growth rate of technology θ.[9] The differences are the 1+a in the change in labor hours term and the presence of a lagged change in output term. Assuming this lagged change term is uncorrelated with Hall's instruments, Hall's estimated markup is not a measure of μ but is actually a measure of $\mu(1+a)$. The difference occurs because a fraction a/(1+a) of the change in labor hours (i.e., marginal cost) is deferred by one period. A change in labor hours appears to be more effective at changing output than it actually is.

In addition, part of what is measured as this period's change in labor hours is due to last period's change in output—hence the lagged change in output term. Another way to interpret the lagged output term is to say that a high lagged increase in output, given this period's change in labor hours, reduces current output, because part of current labor hours are going to pay for the past increase in output. Similarly, a decline in lagged output boosts current output, because the current change in labor hours is net of the decline in hours resulting from last period's decline in output.

In estimating the output equation in his first paper, Hall incorporated the cost of capital into his measure of marginal cost, so that

$$x = \frac{w \Delta N + r \Delta K}{\Delta Q - \theta Q} \, .$$

When this expression is inserted into the calculations above, Hall's output equation (2.11) is changed so that the rate of change of output becomes the rate of change of the output/capital ratio, while the rate of change of the labor/capital ratio takes the place of the rate of change of labor.[10]

How capital should be included in marginal cost is in fact not obvious. In his later paper, Hall revised the equation for marginal cost to read

$$(2.12) \quad x = \frac{w \Delta N + rz \Delta K}{\Delta Q - \theta Q}$$

where z is defined as the "marginal benefit of capital."[11] At this point in the chapter, I impose the constraint z = 0. Thus, in the short run, marginal cost is solely the cost of increased labor hours. This constraint is relaxed, with interesting results, in Section 3.

Revised Markup Estimates

Hall kindly furnished the data necessary for the regressions. All data are annual. The dependent variable is the log change in real GNP, from the N.I.P.A. The labor variable is the log change in hours worked

Table 2.1
Estimated Markups, Accounting for Deferred Marginal Cost

Industry	a	a2	μ	Hall's μ	R^2	D.W.
20 Food and kindred	0.27		1.70	2.34	0.01	1.74
products	(0.22)		(0.85)	(1.14)		
21 Tobacco	0.04		0.87	0.94	0.24	1.66
	(0.19)		(1.67)	(1.59)		
	-0.03	0.09	1.59		0.25	1.26
	(0.18)	(0.17)	(1.47)			
22 Textiles	-0.09		1.17	1.09	0.42	2.01
	(0.14)		(0.34)	(0.26)		
	-0.05	0.18	1.05		0.49	2.18
	(0.15)	(0.15)	(0.30)			
23 Apparel	-0.15		1.47	1.27	0.51	2.17
	(0.14)		(0.39)	(0.24)		
24 Lumber and wood	-0.07		1.14	1.08	0.47	1.91
products	(0.14)		(0.34)	(0.28)		
25 Furniture and	0.14		1.22	1.37	0.85	2.10
fixtures	(0.08)		(0.16)	(0.14)		
26 Paper	0.13		2.66	2.97	0.71	1.32
	(0.11)		(0.48)	(0.46)		
27 Printing and	0.23		1.45	1.77	0.44	1.33
publishing	(0.17)		(0.36)	(0.52)		
28 Chemicals	0.80**		2.19	3.74	0.30	1.11
	(0.25)		(0.52)	(1.29)		
	0.81**	0.30	1.62		0.31	1.08
	(0.25)	(0.20)	(0.47)			
30 Rubber	-0.01		1.43	1.43	0.65	2.38
	(0.12)		(0.27)	(0.19)		
31 Leather	0.20		1.19	1.51	0.44	2.48
	(0.16)		(0.42)	(0.39)		
	0.37*	0.26	0.94		0.54	2.06
	(0.17)	(0.16)	(0.31)			
32 Stone, clay and	0.39**		1.34	1.85	0.88	1.41
glass	(0.07)		(0.12)	(0.23)		
33 Primary metals	0.06		1.96	2.12	0.93	2.04
	(0.05)		(0.19)	(0.14)		
34 Fabricated metals	0.10		1.35	1.51	0.88	1.70
	(0.07)		(0.14)	(0.12)		
35 Nonelectrical	0.07		1.33	1.45	0.90	2.10
machinery	(0.06)		(0.12)	(0.12)		
36 Electrical	0.12		1.34	1.51	0.73	2.20
machinery	(0.11)		(0.19)	(0.19)		

Table 2.1 continues on next page.

Table 2.1 (continued)

Industry	a	a2	μ	Hall's μ	R^2	D.W.
371 Motor vehicles	0.22**		1.74	2.09	0.89	1.72
and parts	(0.07)		(0.20)	(0.23)		
	0.26**	0.08	1.47		0.91	1.71
	(0.06)	(0.06)	(0.19)			
372 Other transportation	-0.20*		1.22	0.92	0.90	2.00
equipment	(0.08)		(0.13)	(0.17)		
38 Instruments	0.20		1.11	1.46	0.72	2.43
	(0.11)		(0.14)	(0.19)		
39 Miscellaneous	0.37**		0.98	1.39	0.57	2.64
manufacturing	(0.12)		(0.20)	(0.28)		
Durable manufacturing	0.18**		1.38	1.67	0.94	1.66
	(0.05)		(0.09)	(0.11)		
Nondurable manufacturing	0.13		1.47	1.66	0.72	1.75
	(0.10)		(0.22)	(0.20)		
All manufacturing	0.18**		1.43	1.72	0.92	1.76
	(0.06)		(0.11)	(0.12)		

Notes: The results shown above were obtained by estimating equation (2.10) using instrumental variables, except for "Hall's μ", which was obtained by estimating equation (2.11). D.W. indicates the Durbin-Watson statistic. "a2" is the coefficient of the second lag of the change in output in the equations in which it was used. * denotes significance of "a" at the 95% level. ** denotes significance of "a" at the 99% level. The regressions used to estimate "Hall's μ" and the regressions with just one lag of the change in output were estimated using annual data for 1950 to 1978, or 1950 to 1972 and 1974 to 1978 for industries undergoing redefinition, as indicated in the text. Regressions with two lags of the change in output were estimated using annual data for 1951 to 1978, or 1951-72 and 1974-78. Figures in parentheses are standard errors.

of all employees, also from the N.I.P.A. Labor share is calculated as compensation of employees divided by nominal GNP, excluding indirect business taxes. The log change of total U.S. real GNP is used as an instrument (as in Hall's work). Certain industries—lumber and wood products (SIC 24), furniture and fixtures (25), chemicals (28), rubber and plastic products (30), primary metals (33), fabricated metals (34), electrical machinery (36), and instruments (38) underwent definitional changes in 1973. Following Hall's lead, the 1973 observations are omitted for these industries.

Hall estimated his equation over the sample period 1949-78. The necessity of including the lagged change in output forces me to change the sample period to 1950-78. Table 2.1 compares the results from estimation of equation (2.10) with the estimated markups derived from Hall's equation (2.11). Both equations are estimated assuming $z = 0$.

In certain industries, full adjustment of labor to output is not completed within the first year after output has changed. In all cases where a second lag of the change in output improved the standard error of the markup estimate, such results are included. (These cases generally correspond to those in which the second lag is nearly significant.) For the rest of the chapter, equation (2.10) is assumed to include a second lag of output for all industries where this condition is met.

As can easily be seen, Hall's estimate of μ—approximately equal to our estimate of μ(1+a)—is biased upward. In several cases, a is significantly positive. We will return to the issue of whether or not this solves the Hall paradox later in the chapter. At this point, we are concerned with demonstrating that marginal costs are deferred. For five two-digit industries, as well as for durable, nondurable and total manufacturing, the deferment is significant at the 99% level. In most other cases, it is statistically insignificant but has the correct sign.

Different Frequencies of Estimation

The existence of deferred marginal cost is also supported if the estimated markups using Hall's specification depend on the frequency of the data used. Since adjustment of labor hours to output takes time, more marginal cost is deferred beyond the quarter in which output changes than the year in which output changes. Hence, the bias in Hall's specification should be greater for quarterly than for annual data. Accounting for deferred marginal cost should reduce this relative bias.

To show this, we must employ alternative measures of labor hours and output, since the series Hall used are available only at annual frequencies. For output, we use the Federal Reserve Board's index of industrial production. Total labor hours are found by multiplying the BLS estimate of the number of employees by its estimate of weekly hours of production workers. Since labor compensation data is not available quarterly, quarterly values for labor compensation as a share of value added were set equal to the annual values.

Results for manufacturing, durable manufacturing and nondurable manufacturing are shown in Table 2.2a. When no lags of output are used, the manufacturing markup estimated with quarterly data is more

Table 2.2a
Estimated Markups, Using Different Frequencies of Estimation

	I	II	III	IV	V	VI
Manufacturing	1.67	1.88	1.49	1.56	1.44	1.42
	(0.09)	(0.09)	(0.08)		(0.11)	
Nondurable	1.68	1.82	1.61	1.75	1.35	1.46
manufacturing	(0.18)	(0.14)	(0.20)		(0.22)	
Durable	1.62	1.84	1.44	1.50	1.49	1.45
manufacturing	(0.08)	(0.08)	(0.07)		(0.10)	

This table shows the estimates of μ obtained by estimating equation (2.10) at both annual and quarterly frequencies using various lag structures on output. The variables used are described in the text. The change in real GNP at the relevant frequency is used as an instrument for the change in labor hours term. Standard errors are in parentheses. The sample period is 1951-78 (or 1951-72, 1974-78).
Column I is estimated using annual data and has no lagged output term. (This is Hall's basic equation (2.11).) Column II employs the same specification but uses quarterly data.
Column III results from estimating equation (2.10), including the lagged output term, using annual data. The regressions producing column IV were run using quarterly data, substituting a second-order pdl of four lags of output for the single lag in the annual equation.
Column V shows the results from estimating equation (2.10) with annual data and two lags of output. Column VI, estimated with quarterly data, utilizes a third order pdl of eight lags of output.

than two standard deviations higher than the estimate obtained using annual data. At the two-digit level, only one manufacturing industry, other transportation equipment, has a higher markup when annual rather than quarterly data is used, and the quarterly markup averages 1.3 standard deviations higher than the annual markup.

The results change markedly when lagged output is introduced into the equation. The third and fourth columns of Table 2.2a compare the results obtained using annual data with one lag of output with those obtained using quarterly data with a pdl of four lags of output. Both estimates of the manufacturing markup are reduced substantially, and the estimate found using quarterly data is only 0.9 standard deviations above the estimate found using annual data. Four two-digit industries have annual markups higher than the quarterly markup, and the average difference for all industries drops to 1.0 standard deviation.

The final two columns of Table 2.2a show that expanding the pdl in the quarterly equation to eight lags actually reduces the estimated

Table 2.2b
Sums of Lagged Output Coefficients, Using Different Frequencies of
Estimation

	III	IV	V	VI
Manufacturing	0.14	0.27	0.17	0.37
	(0.04)	(0.05)	(0.06)	(0.07)
Nondurable	0.06	0.08	0.21	0.30
manufacturing	(0.07)	(0.07)	(0.11)	(0.11)
Durable	0.13	0.29	0.11	0.31
manufacturing	(0.03)	(0.04)	(0.05)	(0.07)

This table shows, for cases III to VI, the sum of coefficients on the lagged output terms—the
parameter a, deferred marginal cost. (For cases I and II, a is assumed to be zero.)

manufacturing markup below that found by adding another lag to the
annual output equation. Although only three industries have annual
markups larger than quarterly markups, the difference between
markups obtained using the two specifications falls to 0.8 standard
deviations.

These equations also provide support for the existence of deferred
marginal cost if the sum of coefficients on the lagged output terms (the
parameter a) is larger at quarterly than at annual frequencies. Indeed,
for both durable manufacturing and for overall manufacturing, the
sum of coefficients on lagged output in the quarterly equations is
several standard deviations above the sum of coefficients in the annual
equation (Table 2.2b). Although the differences are not statistically
significant, more marginal cost is also deferred at a quarterly than at
an annual frequency in nondurable manufacturing.

3. THE MARGINAL BENEFIT OF CAPITAL

We return to the question of how marginal cost is deferred in the
next section of the chapter. In this section, we address the question of
whether deferred marginal cost alone can account for the difference
between the large markups estimated by Hall and the small markups
implied by the actual ratio of value added to costs.

Even though correcting Hall's procedure for deferred marginal
cost reduces the estimated markup for manufacturing from 1.72 to

1.43, this is still significantly larger than the average markup for U.S. manufacturing defined as the ratio of value added to all costs—1.12. Part of the discrepancy is due to the fact that the markup we estimate is a marginal markup—the markup of price over variable costs—which theoretically should equal the ratio of value added to variable costs, a ratio that averaged 1.35 for U.S. manufacturing from 1948 to 1978. In order to estimate something comparable to the average markup, we must redefine marginal cost to include both labor and capital costs. Hence, we must relax the assumption that the marginal benefit of capital, z, equals zero.

In fact, Hall reconciled his high estimated markups with low observed average markups by arguing that the marginal benefit of capital is actually negative. In his paper on capacity utilization, he argued that firms must hold sufficient levels of capacity to reach minimum efficient scales of production. High average profits in a young industry encourage further entry, also at minimum efficient scale, until excess profits are bid away. Because of the requirement that entry must occur at minimum efficient scale, investment decisions are made for discrete amounts of capital, rather than at the margin. Thus, firms may find it profitable to build a plant even if, at the margin, the last increment of investment is worthless.[13] A negative shadow value for capital arises because the excess capital requires overhead labor, thus increasing labor costs.

Hall stated that his empirical finding of a negative shadow value for capital is strongly dependent on the estimated markup.[14] Since our estimates of the markup are quite different than his, it makes sense to reexamine his results. Indeed, using the corrected markup, capital is found to have a positive shadow value.

Hall claimed that the firm has short run cost function

(H1.1) $C(Q, K, w) = wL(Q, K)$,

where w is the wage and L is the labor requirement for production of output Q with capital K.[15] (Equations (H1.1), (H1.2) and so on are taken from Hall's paper and, other than the prefix H, are numbered as they appear there.) He defined the marginal benefit of capital, z, as

(H1.3) $z_t = -\dfrac{w_t}{r_t} \dfrac{\Delta L_t}{\Delta K_t}$, the reduction in the cost of this period's labor requirement needed to hold output constant, given an increase in this period's capital stock, multiplied by its rental price. Thus, z is the dollar change in labor costs per dollar increase in capital costs. The firm minimizes total costs with respect to capital, given some level of output:

$$(\text{H1.2}) \quad \underset{K_t}{\text{MinE}}\left\{\sum_t R_t\left[w_t L_t\left(Q_t, K_t\right) + r_t K_t\right]\right\},$$

where R_t is the discount factor for period t, and E denotes the expectations operator. Rearranging the first order conditions yields

$$(\text{H1.4}) \quad E(z_t) = 1.$$

Ideally, the rental cost of a unit of capital should equal the amount of labor costs which are saved because of its use. Hall's estimate of z_t in manufacturing, however, is −0.93, so he concluded that firms hold capacity far in excess of what is needed to minimize costs at the margin. Such behavior by firms is rational in his model, however, because capital stock decisions are not made at the margin.

Since Hall's empirical results depend strongly on high estimated markups, they will be altered once we take deferred marginal cost into account. In addition, his first order condition for the shadow value of capital, equation (H1.4), holds only when firms are continually operating at capacity. We have three goals here: (1) to show that our a priori expectation of the marginal benefit of capital should not be one, as Hall claimed, but a value between zero and one; (2) to modify Hall's technique of measuring the marginal benefit of capital to take deferred marginal cost into account; (3) to show that, correctly measured, the marginal benefit of capital is indeed between zero and one.

Equation (H1.4) holds only if short run changes in the capital stock alter the amount of labor required to produce output Q. In the long run, this is of course true, since capital is fully flexible. Suppose, however, that in the short run, the existing effective capital/effective labor ratio cannot be altered, i.e., assume ex post fixed proportions. Old equipment cannot be adjusted so as to require less labor per unit capital, while new equipment requires labor in similar proportions as existing capital, subject to technological improvements. The labor requirement to produce any given output thus has nothing to do with short run changes in the capital stock, unless firms are operating at capacity. Therefore, in all cases but full capacity,

(2.13) $E(z_t) = 0$.

At capacity, Hall's equation (H1.4) continues to hold. In fact, one can generate Hall's (H1.4) as the steady state solution by excluding K as an argument from L in equation (H1.1) and adding production constraints to the minimization problem (H1.2).

Hall used two methods to construct z, the marginal benefit of capital. These must be altered to take account of deferred marginal cost. The first method Hall used was to estimate $\bar{z}$, average z, using the two-equation system described below. The second was to create a time series by calculating z_t for each year. In Hall's case, as well as mine, the two procedures give answers consistent with one another. However, while Hall found z to be significantly negative, I find it to be significantly positive.

We now outline Hall's procedure for generating a system of two equations by which $\bar{z}$ can be estimated.[16] At the same time, we revise his procedure in light of deferred marginal cost, to provide a more correct measure of $\bar{z}$.

Equation (H1.1), the short run cost function, is changed to read

(2.14) $C(Q, Q_{-1}, K, w) = wL(Q, Q_{-1}, K)$,

where subscripts denote shifts of time period. Constant returns to scale tell us that

(2.15) $\dfrac{Q}{N}\dfrac{\partial L}{\partial Q} + \dfrac{Q_{-1}}{N}\dfrac{\partial L}{\partial Q_{-1}} + \dfrac{K}{N}\dfrac{\partial L}{\partial K} = 1$.

(Hall used L to refer to the labor requirement and N to refer to actual labor hours. He eventually set the two equal.) Ignoring lagged output, as in the original,

(H1.6) $\dfrac{Q}{N}\dfrac{\partial L}{\partial Q} + \dfrac{K}{N}\dfrac{\partial L}{\partial K} = 1$.

In Hall's paper, marginal cost is

(H1.7) $x = w\dfrac{\partial L}{\partial Q}$.

In our case, assuming that this year's real wage equals the expectation of next year's real wage times the discount factor, as in equation (2.2), marginal cost is

$$(2.16) \quad x = w \frac{\partial L}{\partial Q} + w \frac{\partial L_{+1}}{\partial Q} .$$

Hall then substituted equation (H1.7) into equation (H1.6) and combined this with equation (H1.3) to get

$$(H1.8) \quad z = \frac{xQ - wN}{rK} .$$

Inserting his definition of marginal cost,

$$(2.12) \quad x = \frac{w \Delta N + rz \Delta K}{\Delta Q - \theta Q} ,$$

into this equation, Hall could then solve for z:

$$(H1.11) \quad z = \frac{\alpha *}{1 - \alpha *} \frac{\Delta n + \theta - \Delta q}{\Delta q - \theta} ,$$

where

$$(H1.12) \quad \alpha * = \frac{wN}{wN + rK} ,$$

Δn is the proportional rate of change of the labor-capital ratio and Δq is the proportional rate of change of the output-capital ratio.

Some algebraic manipulation of equation (1.11) produces

$$(H1.14) \quad \frac{1}{1 - \alpha *} (\Delta q - \alpha * \Delta n) = (1 - \bar{z}) \Delta q + \frac{1}{1 - \alpha *} \theta$$
$$- (1 - \bar{z}) \theta - (\Delta q - \theta) \varepsilon,$$

where ε is the mean zero disturbance of z and $\bar{z}$ is the mean of z. Redefining θ to be the constant component of technological progress, Hall estimated the two equation system consisting of (H1.14) and (2.11). The error component of (H1.14) is correlated with Δq but not with demand, so the change in GNP is used as an instrument.

This two equation system was estimated using the nonlinear three-stage least squares technique of Amemiya.[19] The result for equation (H1.14) for total manufacturing was

$$\text{(H1.14)} \quad \frac{1}{1-\alpha^*}(\Delta q - \alpha^* \Delta n) = (1 - \underset{(0.24)}{0.93})\Delta q + \frac{1}{1-\alpha^*}\underset{(0.004)}{0.035}$$
$$-\underset{(0.24)}{(1.93)}\underset{(0\,004)}{(0.035)},$$

where the numbers in parentheses below the coefficients are standard errors.[18] The estimated value of $\overline{z}$, the marginal benefit of capital, is −0.93, with a standard error of 0.24. Thus, the marginal benefit of capital is significantly negative.

In deriving his output equation, Hall assumed $z = 1$. Once this assumption is relaxed, however, the output equation is incorrectly specified. To accurately measure $\overline{z}$, we must thus create a two equation system which both corrects this problem and accounts for deferred marginal cost.

Converting (2.16), the revised definition of marginal cost, to elasticities, we have

$$\text{(2.17)} \quad x = \frac{wL}{Q}\frac{\partial L/L}{\partial Q/Q} + \frac{wL_{+1}}{Q}\frac{\partial L_{+1}/L_{+1}}{\partial Q/Q}.$$

Using as an approximation $E(L_{+1}) = L$, setting $L = N$, and noting that by shifting time periods

$$\text{(2.18)} \quad \frac{\partial L_{+1}/L_{+1}}{\partial Q/Q} = \frac{\partial L/L}{\partial Q_{-1}/Q_{-1}},$$

we can substitute (2.17) into (2.15) to get

$$\text{(2.19)} \quad \frac{xQ}{wN} + \frac{K}{N}\frac{\partial L}{\partial K} = 1.$$

In combination with (H1.3), we can solve for z:

$$\text{(2.20)} \quad z = \frac{xQ - wN}{rK}.$$

This is identical to equation (H1.8).

We now want to substitute for x in this equation. Modify equation (2.12) so that it now reads

$$\text{(2.21)} \quad x = \frac{w\Delta N_{t,t} + w\Delta N_{t+1,t} + rz\Delta K_t}{\Delta Q_t - \theta Q_t}.$$

Following the same procedure which produced equation (2.8) in Section 2, we find that

$$(2.22) \quad x = \frac{w(1+a)\Delta N_t + rz(\Delta K_t + a\Delta K_{t-1})}{\Delta Q_t - \theta Q_t + a\Delta Q_{t-1} - a\theta Q_{t-1}}.$$

This expression is substituted into equation (2.20). After considerable algebraic manipulation, we can replace (H1.14) with

$$(2.23)$$
$$\frac{1}{1-\alpha*}(\Delta q - \alpha*\Delta n) = (1-\bar{z})(\Delta q + aq_{-1}) + \frac{1+a}{1-\alpha*}\theta$$
$$-(1+a)(1-\bar{z})\theta$$
$$-\frac{a}{1-\alpha*}(\Delta q_{-1} - \alpha*\Delta n_{-1})$$
$$+\frac{a\alpha*}{1-\alpha*}(\frac{\Delta N}{N} - \frac{\Delta N_{-1}}{N_{-1}}) + \varepsilon,$$

where ε is an error term correlated with increases in output but uncorrelated with demand. (To see the resemblance between (2.23) and (H1.14), multiply through the latter by (1+a) and move the lagged Solow residual term to the right-hand side. The only remaining difference results from the lack of a lagged change in labor hours term in (2.22).)

Equation (2.23) is one of the two equations to be estimated. Because equation (2.10) ignores the role of capital in marginal cost, it must be modified before it can be used as the other equation in the two-equation system. Using (2.22) in place of (2.8) in the procedure used to derive equation (2.10) in Section 2, we find that

$$(2.24) \quad \Delta q_t = \mu\frac{w_t N_t}{P_t Q_t}(1+a)\Delta n_t - a\Delta q_{t-1} + (1+a)\theta$$

$$-a\mu\frac{w_t N_t}{P_t Q_t}(\Delta k_t - \Delta k_{t-1}) - (1-\bar{z})\mu\frac{r_t K_t}{P_t Q_t}(\Delta k_t + a\Delta k_{t-1}),$$

where Δq is the proportional rate of change of the output-capital ratio, Δn is the proportional rate of change of the labor-capital ratio and Δk is the proportional rate of change of capital. In the estimation of this equation, the rate of change of real GNP is used as an instrument for Δn.

Table 2.3
Average Marginal Benefit of Capital, From Joint Estimation of
Equations (2.23) and (2.24)

Industry	a	μ	$\overline{z}$	R^2
20 Food and kindred	0.22	1.14	-0.27	0.02
products	(0.14)	(0.11)	(0.40)	
21 Tobacco	-0.66##	1.28	-5.01##	0.09
	(0.11)	(0.11)	(0.36)	
22 Textiles	-0.92##	0.28	-4.87##	0.05
	(0.08)	(0.36)	(0.27)	
23 Apparel	0.19#	0.74	-8.64##	0.45
	(0.07)	(0.16)	(2.58)	
24 Lumber and wood	-0.97##	0.48	-6.38##	0.02
products	(0.04)	(0.38)	(0.19)	
25 Furniture and	-0.88##	0.28	-10.70##	0.00
fixtures	(0.09)	(0.27)	(0.55)	
26 Paper	0.16	1.15	-0.67##	0.72
	(0.08)	(0.18)	(0.21)	
27 Printing and	-0.98##	1.57	-8.24##	0.00
publishing	(0.07)	(0.67)	(0.63)	
28 Chemicals	-0.78##	2.09	-2.45##	0.00
	(0.08)	(0.40)	(0.10)	
30 Rubber	-0.72##	1.08	-4.88##	0.01
	(0.08)	(0.43)	(0.33)	
31 Leather	0.17*	1.05	-2.79	0.43
	(0.07)	(0.25)	(2.26)	
32 Stone, clay and	0.37**	1.27	0.36**	0.90
glass	(0.05)	(0.04)	(0.12)	
33 Primary metals	0.11**	1.32	-0.32#	0.92
	(0.03)	(0.09)	(0.12)	
34 Fabricated metals	0.08	1.18	0.25	0.89
	(0.04)	(0.06)	(0.25)	
35 Nonelectrical	0.07	1.22	0.50**	0.90
machinery	(0.04)	(0.03)	(0.12)	
36 Electrical	0.11	1.20	0.45	0.75
machinery	(0.08)	(0.06)	(0.29)	
371 Motor vehicles	0.23**	1.49	-0.47#	0.90
and parts	(0.04)	(0.10)	(0.22)	
372 Other transportation	-0.26##	1.08	0.47	0.90
equipment	(0.05)	(0.06)	(0.27)	
38 Instruments	0.12	1.20	0.23	0.78
	(0.08)	(0.03)	(0.16)	
39 Miscellaneous	0.19*	1.18	0.29	0.54
manufacturing	(0.09)	(0.06)	(0.31)	

Table 2.3 continues on next page.

Table 2.3 (continued)

Industry	a	μ	z̄	R^2
Durable manufacturing	0.19**	1.23	0.37*	0.94
	(0.04)	(0.04)	(0.14)	
Nondurable manufacturing	0.17*	1.21	0.33	0.72
	(0.07)	(0.06)	(0.17)	
All manufacturing	0.21**	1.23	0.31*	0.92
	(0.04)	(0.05)	(0.15)	

Notes: Each system of two equations was estimated with three stage least squares, as discussed in the text. Equations were estimated with only one lag of output. R^2 is for equation (2.24), rearranged so that Δq is the dependent variable (for comparison to the R^2 in Table 2.1). * means significantly positive at the 95% level. ** means significantly positive at the 99% level. # means significantly negative at the 95% level. ## means significantly negative at the 99% level. The regressions were estimated using annual data for 1950-78, or 1950-72 and 1974-78 in cases where the industry definition changed. Figures in parentheses are standard errors.

Data for the U.S. manufacturing sector are provided by Hall.[19] wN is compensation of all employees and pQ is nominal value added. The joint system of equations (2.23) and (2.24) was estimated using Amemiya's three-stage least squares procedure (Table 2.3).

For aggregate manufacturing, the most significant deviation from Hall's results is that z̄ is now significantly positive. The value, 0.31, is consistent with my theory that z equals one only when firms operate at full capacity and zero otherwise, and means that the capital constraint is binding 31% of the time.

The coefficient *a* is significantly positive, once again furnishing evidence that firms do desire to defer some marginal costs of changing production. Another interesting result is that the markup is now only 1.23, smaller than the 1.43 from estimating equation (2.10) alone and much smaller than the 1.72 found using Hall's original equation.

Overall, the results for durable and nondurable manufacturing are remarkably similar to those for total manufacturing. Similar results are obtained for stone, clay and glass, fabricated metals, nonelectrical machinery, electrical machinery, instruments, and miscellaneous manufacturing. In all these cases, z̄ is between 0.23 and 0.50, *a* is positive and occasionally significant, and the markup is between 1.18 and 1.27. For other transportation equipment, *a* is significantly negative and the markup is only 1.08, but z̄ falls in the same range as the industries listed above. For primary metals, z̄ is small but

Table 2.4
Marginal Benefit of Capital in Manufacturing, Calculated Using
Alternative Estimated Markups

	Markup		
	1.23	1.43	1.67[a]
1950	0.73	0.00	-0.64
1951	0.79	0.01	-0.66
1952	0.58	-0.19	-0.86
1953	0.49	-0.23	-0.95
1954	0.46	-0.31	-0.98
1955	0.72	-0.15	-0.91
1956	0.51	-0.29	-0.99
1957	0.43	-0.31	-0.95
1958	0.32	-0.39	-1.00
1959	0.55	-0.26	-0.97
1960	0.40	-0.38	-1.06
1961	0.41	-0.39	-1.00
1962	0.53	-0.35	-1.12
1963	0.66	-0.26	-1.07
1964	0.73	-0.24	-1.08
1965	0.90	-0.08	-0.95
1966	0.78	-0.13	-0.93
1967	0.62	-0.24	-0.99
1968	0.61	-0.25	-1.00
1969	0.38	-0.37	-1.02
1970	0.18	-0.44	-0.98
1971	0.34	-0.34	-0.94
1972	0.39	-0.34	-0.98
1973	0.34	-0.39	-1.03
1974	0.13	-0.47	-0.99
1975	0.28	-0.28	-0.78
1976	0.38	-0.25	-0.80
1977	0.41	-0.21	-0.76
1978	0.34	-0.23	-0.94
sample			
average	0.50	-0.27	-0.94

[a] Source: Robert Hall, "Chronic Excess Capacity in U.S. Industry," NBER Working Paper 1973, July 1986, 23.

significantly negative, although the markup drops to 1.32 from 1.96 in equation (2.10). Food, paper and motor vehicles are also industries where the markup is a reasonable size, a is positive, but $\overline{z}$ is slightly negative.

Unfortunately, results for the remaining industries are implausible. Estimates of $\bar{z}$ range from -2.79 in leather products to an impossible -10.70 in furniture and fixtures. Estimates of the markup are frequently less than one, and generally have large standard errors. The overall fit for these equations is very poor, however: for all but one of these industries, the R^2 for equation (2.24) is virtually zero.

The second method Hall used to determine z, the marginal benefit of capital, is algebraically much simpler. Using the definition of μ, he rearranged equation (H1.8) to get

$$(H1.9) \quad z = \frac{(1/\mu)pQ - wN}{rK} \quad,$$

where pQ and wN are defined above. rK, given by Hall,[20] is the rental cost of capital, constructed following the method of Hall and Jorgenson.[21] Using the value of 1.67 for μ that he estimated in his original paper, Hall found values of z ranging from -0.64 in 1950 to -1.12 in 1962 (Table 2.4). These values are consistent with his three stage least squares estimate for z of -0.93.

Since equation (H1.8) holds in our case as well in Hall's, so does equation (H1.9). Calculated z for aggregate manufacturing, using the markups of 1.23 estimated in the revised system of equations and 1.43 estimated using equation (2.10), are shown next to Hall's calculated values in Table 2.4. The sample average for the 1950-78 period using a markup of 1.23 is 0.50, somewhat higher than $\bar{z}$ as estimated in the two equation system. The pattern exhibited by z indicates that our interpretation of it as a measure of capacity constraints is close to the mark: the series reaches its cyclical peak the same year as the capacity utilization rate in manufacturing twice, and in the previous year twice. Only in 1951-53 and 1977-79 are peaks in the series two years apart. These results should be interpreted with caution, however, both because the sample average differs from estimated $\bar{z}$ and because equation (H1.9) assumes a constant value for μ. Failure to account for variability of μ will introduce spurious movements in z as calculated using equation (H1.9).

To sum up, the two equation system formed by equations (2.24) and (2.23) indicates that z, the marginal benefit of capital as defined by Hall, is significantly positive. This result refutes Hall's contention that excess profits are bid away by excess capacity. Nonetheless, Hall's basic result—that markups are surprisingly large—still holds: even the relatively small markup produced by the two equation system above, 1.23, is still significantly larger than value added divided by total costs, 1.12.

What, then, can explain the difference between marginal and average markups? The puzzle is this: when capital is not being fully utilized, the only cost of increasing production is the cost of increased labor hours. Why do firms not take advantage of the low marginal cost of production in recessions by reducing prices and producing to capacity? This is the real significance of Hall's results; firms would only fail to produce at capacity in a recession if they had enough market power that such actions would mean drastic reductions in price.

The data seem to indicate that firms act as if capital were costly to use, even with output below capacity, i.e., firms act as if the marginal benefit of capital, z, is always unity. Indeed, this must be true, since setting $z = 1$ means that equation (H1.9) can be rearranged to form

$$(2.25) \quad \mu = \frac{pQ}{wN + rK} ,$$

meaning the marginal and average markups are equal. Thus, our query can also be posed as follows: why do firms behave as if an increase in output, even when output is below capacity, will require an increase in capital costs in addition to an increase in labor costs? Rather than searching for evidence of market power, research on Hall's finding should try to answer why firms act as if the utilization of idle capital is costly. If one can explain why this is true, one can explain the Hall puzzle.

Two possible explanations follow. Both explanations expand the notion of deferred marginal cost from labor to capital, so that a current increase in output involves not only a current increase in capital but an increase in the future as well.

One possibility, suggested by Epstein and Denny, is that greater utilization results in wear and tear on the machinery and thus hastens the day when it must be replaced.[22] Suppose capital is used until it is physically obsolescent, so that any piece of capital is used until it has been employed a given number of hours, and then can be used no longer. Then depreciation of capital depends on the amount of time it has been used, rather than on how old it is. Marginal variable cost, then, includes not only the change in labor hours, but also the use of capital incurred by those labor hours. By not including this, our estimates of marginal cost are biased down. Such a bias, coupled with the failure to take deferred marginal cost into consideration, would account for the difference between the estimated and actual average markups.

A second possible explanation why firms view an increase in output as causing an increase in capital costs, even when production is below capacity, involves a distinction between long-run and short-run elasticities of demand. Assume customer markets in the style of Okun, in which the sale of a good to a customer establishes a long-term buyer-seller relationship with that customer.[23] In such a situation, any customers a firm adds are viewed as permanent customers, especially if customers only switch sellers when a price cut is viewed as permanent. In determining the net gain of adding new customers, the firm must take account of current and future added revenues and costs.

Now assume that the firm has just enough capacity to satisfy its existing customers at peak demand. (The argument also holds when the firm has insufficient capacity.) By adding new customers in a recession, the firm is implicitly committing itself to build new capacity when demand recovers. Thus, the shadow cost of selling to additional customers in a recession is not just the cost of an increase in labor hours, but includes the cost of the capital that will eventually be installed in order to satisfy the new customers. Firms act as if marginal cost includes this cost of capital, even though no increase in capital would occur at the time of the increase in output.

4. EVIDENCE FOR VARYING LEVELS OF EFFORT

Having shown that a substantial component of the excess markups observed by Hall result from the failure to account for deferred marginal costs, we now turn to the question of how such costs are deferred.

The second section of the chapter showed that, when faced with a demand-induced increase in output, the firm will defer part of the corresponding increase in inputs to later periods. (Similarly, when demand and output fall, the firm will postpone part of the reduction in inputs that is made possible.) Assuming constant returns to scale, however, an increase in labor hours which is less than proportional to the increase in output is a violation of the production function, unless some factor which affects the productivity of labor is increasing simultaneously. The remainder of this chapter assumes that a third input to production—effort—makes up the difference between changes in output and changes in labor hours. (Another possible explanation for output increasing more rapidly than labor hours, not examined here but suggested by Solow, is that the intensity of capital usage, as well as the amount of capital used, varies procyclically.)[24]

We will assume that workers vary their effort according to an implicit contract they have with the firm. This idea has its precedent in work by George Akerlof:

> According to standard theory, when a firm hires a laborer, there is an understanding by both parties that certain minimum standards of performance must be met. Furthermore, the contract may be implicit in the sense that workers need not be currently rewarded for their current performance but may earn chances for promotion with higher pay in the future in return for good performance in their current jobs. If this is the case, the firm need not have tight rules regarding work and compensation that very carefully specify the quid pro quo of pay for work, since injustices in the present can be compensated later.[25]

But the reward need not take the form of a promotion or increase in pay:

> With the cash posters (or any other work group whose effort is determined not by the work rules but by the group's norms) the question arises: What does the group receive in return for working more than prescribed by the work rules? In the first place the worker may receive leniency in the work rules. Even if the worker habitually works at a speed in excess of work rules, he still benefits from leniency in two ways. First, he derives positive utility from the gift by the firm of potential leniency should he slacken his pace; . . . [26]

Under the implicit contracts discussed in this chapter, the workers will "work more than prescribed by the work rules" in a certain way: in periods of increasing demand, workers will increase their effort so that the firm can meet the extra demand. The "leniency" of the firm may take either of two forms. In the first case, discussed in Section 5, the firm compensates its workers for extra effort expended by reducing effort below the norm in the future. Thus, over time the level of effort will average out to the norm set when the workers enter into the implicit contract. In the second case, discussed in Section 6, workers receive leniency to work less in periods of falling demand. The difference between the two cases is that in the second, there is no need for the amounts of extra and subnormal effort to balance each other out ex post. Workers agree at the time of employment to adjust effort to demand so that in expectation, effort will equal the norm. In actuality, however, effort will likely average either above or below the norm.

Anecdotal evidence that workers have the freedom to set their effort levels is provided by Akerlof:

> . . . Burawoy's workers [at a piecework machine shop] have considerable freedom in the operation of their machines and in their complex interactions with other workers. If they choose to produce less, they can do so; . . . Thus workers would have no difficulty in decreasing their output if they so desired while still abiding by the rules.[27]

The remainder of this section: (1) answers the three objections Hall raised against the idea of cyclically varying effort; (2) answers the question of why firms would want such a contract in the first place; (3) answers the question of why the repayment feature of the contract would not take a different form, such as concurrent variations in the wage rate.

Hall himself suggested the possibility that procyclical variations in work effort might bias his results:

> Of the various specification errors that may have biased the estimate of the markup ratio upward, the only one that seems to have the potential to reverse the conclusion of chronic excess capacity is the following, considered at length in the earlier paper: There are unmeasured variations in work effort that are positively correlated with output. A proper measure of marginal cost would count the cost of extra effort and might reverse the conclusion that marginal cost is well under price.[28]

However, he then stated three objections to the idea: (1) the magnitude of the fluctuations in effort would have to be "large"; (2) "survey evidence collected from employers by Fay and Medoff (1985) suggests that effort is slightly negatively correlated with output"; (3) wages fail to move enough to compensate workers for changes in effort.[29]

Regarding the first point, it is difficult to tell what "large" means. Hall estimated that effort never deviates by more than 9% from its normal level, assuming that changes in effort have the same effect on output as changes in labor.[30] Hall's method of calculation imparts an upward bias to this estimate, however, because it assumes that labor hours affect output only in proportion to labor's share of revenue, rather than one-to-one, as under ex post fixed proportions. Hall's method thus overstates the change in effort needed to produce a given change in output. The maximum deviation in effort is actually 6-7%, not 9%. Are such variations in effort "large"? They do not appear to be.

Concerning Hall's second criticism, the point of the Fay and Medoff paper is not to measure effort, but to demonstrate labor hoarding, which they do. Effort is only discussed as a way in which labor may be hoarded, a discussion which occupies just two paragraphs of the paper. Fay and Medoff asked respondents—plant managers—to rate average blue-collar worker effort relative to "normal" at various points in the business cycle. They admit that "Because the measure of effort is crude, the evidence regarding effort must be viewed as only suggestive." Indeed, the evidence seems inconclusive, with 30% of all firms which hoard labor reporting increased effort between the peak and trough of the cycle, 39% reporting unchanged effort, and 31% reporting reduced effort. Almost one-third of all firms surveyed thus exhibit procyclical effort.[31]

For the purpose of measuring effort over the course of the business cycle, Shea's paper seems more appropriate. Instead of a subjective assessment of workers' effort by their managers, the paper uses observable variables which should be tied to effort. In addition, unlike the Fay and Medoff results, Shea's results are unambiguous, pointing to significantly procyclical effort.[32]

Finally, remember that both the Shea and the Fay and Medoff studies cover only blue collar workers. Labor hours of nonproduction workers respond more slowly to changes in output than do hours of production workers, indicating that the amount of marginal cost deferred, and thus the magnitude of fluctuations in effort, is larger for this group.

Regarding Hall's third criticism, compensation for effort need not take the form of an increase in wages. The firm may "repay" the workers by allowing them to reduce their effort in the future, as the second quote from Akerlof suggests. This notion of intertemporal substitution of effort underlies the model in Section 5 of this chapter. As I discuss below, liquidity-constrained workers will prefer variations in work effort to variations in pay.

Before discussing the form the implicit contract should take, it is necessary to explain why firms and workers desire to allow variations in effort at all, and why an implicit contract governing such variations should exist. Firms desire variations in effort in order to reduce the adjustment costs of changing labor hours. Okun suggested that such adjustment costs result from contractual commitments, transactions costs, the value of holding an inventory of certain skills which might be needed quickly in a upturn, and the adverse effects of labor adjustment on morale.[33] Fair added reorganization costs.[34] Most of these are costs of adjusting labor downward, although an inventory of skills is only valuable if such skills are hard to attract on short notice in a boom, i.e., if there are adjustment costs to increasing the number of workers. The cost of adjusting hours per worker upward is overtime costs. An implicit contract allowing the firm to shift effort between time periods enables the firm to spread out any necessary labor adjustments, the costs of which Solow specified as substantially increasing on the margin.[35]

If effort is a variable under the control of the firm, there must be some cost to utilizing it—otherwise, the firm would use as much of it as possible all the time, not just when demand is high. This cost is specified by the implicit contract, in which workers agree to provide greater than normal levels of effort now in exchange for less than normal levels in the future. Alternatively, if the firm reduces effort now, it can expect to be repaid with higher effort in the future.

Finally, why are current changes in effort offset by future changes in effort, rather than by current changes in the wage rate? The answer is, simply, that liquidity-constrained workers (workers whose income is temporarily too low to finance their desired level of consumption, and whose ability to borrow is limited) prefer fluctuations in effort to fluctuations in income. While the disutility of an extra unit of effort roughly equals the utility added by reducing effort one unit, the disutility of a dollar less in income will exceed the utility of an extra dollar of income once the liquidity constraint is hit.

5. OFFSETTING VARIATIONS IN EFFORT

In this section of the chapter, I explicitly model labor demand for a firm which has an implicit contract with its workers under which it must offset current deviations from the normal level of effort with future deviations in the opposite direction. The firm minimizes labor costs, which include total wages and labor adjustment costs, subject to some output constraint. (Making output exogenous is a simplification —the model becomes much more complicated but still works if demand, rather than output, is exogenous and the firm maximizes profits. Because of the duality of cost minimization and profit maximization, the relationship between effort and output is the same in both cases.) The firm uses the implicit contract to substitute effort across time in order to reduce adjustment costs. For example, if the firm desires to increase current output, an increase in current effort will reduce the size of the adjustment in hours needed this period, and therefore adjustment costs. To compensate workers for this increase in current effort, the firm must reduce effort at some point in the future. Given future output, the reduction in future effort means an increase in future hours. Thus, the firm shifts labor hours across time via intertemporal substitution of effort.

Although we use the term "intertemporal substitution" and have procyclical productivity, this model is quite different from a real business cycle model such as that of Kydland and Prescott. In their model, productivity shocks cause workers to shift labor and firms to shift investment toward periods of greater productivity. The shocks are exogenous, and drive the business cycle.[36] In the model of this chapter, however, firms desire to shift production toward periods of high demand, which can increase for reasons other than productivity shocks. Since adjustment of labor hours is costly, firms will increase (decrease) effort during periods when output is increasing (decreasing). A change in effort produces a change in measured labor productivity, so demand shocks produce fluctuations in labor productivity. The business cycle drives productivity, reversing the direction of causality postulated by Kydland and Prescott.

In this section, an arbitrary form is chosen for the repayment scheme by which deviations in effort are repaid. A different form would produce a somewhat different pattern of labor demand. The only constraint on such an implicit contract imposed by the theory is that workers' utility be at least as high as under a non-varying effort contract. For the particular contract specified, this is verified in an appendix. The question whether the firm is at least as well off is answered if the firm decides to vary effort. Since, under a varying effort contract, the firm could still keep effort constant, then by revealed preference the firm must be at least as well off when it allows effort to vary.

Given an effort-repayment contract, an equation for the change in labor hours demanded is then derived, assuming that the firm minimizes costs taking the contract into account. This labor demand equation helps explain a puzzling empirical result—Robert Gordon's "end-of-expansion" phenomenon, in which labor hours are unusually high after output has been expanding for some period of time.[37] The high labor hours are simply the result of an accumulation of effort during periods of rising output which must be repaid with lower effort (higher hours) later on.

I assume that the labor input into production is "effective" hours, the product of actual labor hours and labor effort. Due to ex post fixed proportions between effective capital and effective hours, there is a proportional relationship between output and effective hours. I define effective labor hours during period t, L^*_t, as

$$(2.26) \quad L^*_t = L_t E_t \, ,$$

where L is actual labor hours and E is effort, determined as an identity given actual and effective hours.

Effort consists of two components:

$$(2.27) \quad E_t = F_t X_t^{-1} \, .$$

F_t, "discretionary effort," is the control variable of the firm, the component of effort which the firm chooses directly. The repayment of effort is captured by the variable X_t, which can be interpreted as the "effort debt" of the firm to its workers.

This section assumes that X_t takes the form

$$(2.28) \quad X_t = 1 + 0.5 \sum_{i=1}^{N} y_i (1 + \log F_{t-i})^2 \frac{L^*_{t-i}}{L^*_t} - 0.5 \sum_{i=1}^{N} y_i \frac{L^*_{t-i}}{L^*_t},$$

where the y_i are time-invariant. F, discretionary effort, is normalized so that in steady state (or on average), it equals 1. By inspection of equation (2.28), the steady state value of X must thus also be 1. The equation states that an increase in current effort, E, due to an increase in current F will boost future X. Equation (2.27) shows that this in turn lowers future effort.

The firm's effort decision can also be modelled without breaking effort into two components. Because of the multi-period nature of the model, however, it is difficult to derive a labor demand function from the first order conditions. Separating effort into its discretionary and repayment components enables us to generate an estimable function for labor hours, while retaining the theoretical implications of the "simpler" model.

Equation (2.28) is a viable implicit contract if it generates at least as much utility as a constant-effort contract. Appendix A shows that, starting from steady state, this is true if: (2A.1) workers' effort disutility is logarithmic in effort; (2A.2) the firm agrees not to let the F_{t+i} explode (a Ponzi scheme in effort); and

$$(2A.3) \quad \sum_{i=1}^{N} R^i y_i = 1.$$

Thus, starting from a position in which there is no positive or negative effort debt, the workers would be willing to accept the contract specified in equation (2.28) over a constant-effort contract.

The only case in which a worker is made worse off by entering into the implicit contract is when the workers already employed by the firm have an effort debt to the firm, i.e., X_t is less than 1. In such a case, the incoming worker may average higher effort under the varying effort contract because he helps to repay the effort debt owed by incumbent workers to the firm. To give these workers as much utility as a constant effort contract would give them, the firm could offer them higher pay (through a higher initial wage or through overtime work) or let them work less hard than incumbent workers while the effort debt is paid off.

Combining equations (2.26) and (2.27), we have

(2.29) $L_t = L*_t X_t F_t^{-1}$.

The ratio of output to effective labor is, at any point in time, constant over the possible range of output due to the assumption of ex post fixed proportions between effective labor hours and effective capital. Thus, $L*_t$, effective labor hours, are determined by output. (Remember that we have assumed output to be exogenous.)

Suppose the firm unanticipatedly desires to increase L* above the level attained last period, either temporarily or permanently. In the absence of varying effort, the firm would do this by increasing actual labor hours proportionately to output, thereby incurring adjustment costs. The firm can reduce these adjustment costs (and, if the increase is known to be temporary, reduce the adjustment costs of returning labor hours to the original level) by partially offsetting the increase in L with an increase in the discretionary component of effort, F. In future periods, however, this extra effort must be repaid by the firm to its workers according to equation (2.28). X in future periods will thus increase, causing labor hours in those future periods to be higher, ceteris paribus. Effort, E, is thus shifted from future periods toward the present, while labor hours are shifted in the other direction—intertemporal substitution of effort and labor hours.

The firm desires to minimize the present discounted value of its labor costs, given present effective labor hours and expectations of future effective labor hours. These costs consist of wage payments and labor adjustment costs. An increase in current labor hours will increase this period's wage payments. Given effective hours, however, the increase in actual hours, ceteris paribus, represents a reduction in effort, which means future wage payments will fall. In addition, an incremental increase in labor hours will mean an increase or decrease in adjustment costs, depending on whether labor hours are already increasing or decreasing.

Mathematically, these labor costs can be represented as

(2.30) $C_t = \sum_{i=0}^{\infty} R^i w_{t+i} L_{t+i} + 0.5 \sum_{i=0}^{\infty} R^i \phi_{t+i} J_{t+i}^2 L*_{t+i}$,

where R is a real discount factor, assumed constant over time, w is real labor compensation per hour, and

(2.31) $J_{t+i} = \log L_{t+i} - \log L_{t+i-1}$.

As stated above, we assume that L*, effective labor hours, are given. The first right hand side term in equation (2.30) simply represents the discounted wage stream. The second term represents quadratic labor adjustment costs. These costs, outlined in Section 4, basically consist of hiring and firing costs and overtime pay. L^*_{t+1} is added to this term to guarantee long-run constant returns to scale. The ϕ_{t+i} are measured in the same units as the w_{t+1}. In fact, because external costs of adjustment will depend strongly on the wage rate, we can simplify the math by using the approximation:

(2.32) $\phi_{t+i} = w_{t+i}\phi_0$.

It is not my purpose in this chapter to show the effects that a change in the discount rate or an expected change in the wage rate have on the intertemporal substitution of effort by the firm. I thus make the simplifying assumption that real wages are a random walk with drift, unconditional on current realizations of L* or L. To simplify the algebra, we use the special case where the "drift" is equal to the rate of time preference:

(2.33) $w_{t+i} = (1/R)w_{t+i-1} + \varepsilon_t$.

According to the model, if firms expect the price of labor to increase in the future, they will want to use more labor now. They can do this by decreasing effort now (increasing hours), and demanding higher effort when the wage increases (reducing hours). The simplifications thus ignore the positive impact of expected increases in the wage and low interest rates on labor demand. This is reasonable, however, since workers will not agree to an implicit contract in which their utility is lower than in a fixed-effort contract. If the firm were to increase hours while wages were low so that hours could be reduced when wages rise, utility would be lower than if no such tradeoff in hours had taken place, so workers would not abide by such an implicit contract.

Substituting equations (2.29) and (2.32) into equation (2.30), we have

$$C_t = w_t L_t + \sum_{i=1}^{\infty} R^i w_{t+i} L^*_{t+i} X_{t+i} F_{t+i}^{-1}$$

(2.34)

$$+0.5 \sum_{i=0}^{\infty} R^i w_{t+i} \phi_0 J_{t+i}^2 L^*_{t+i}.$$

The firm desires to minimize these costs with respect to current labor hours, L_t, realizing that J_t, J_{t+1}, and the X_{t+i} are functions of L_t.

It is now easy to see why assumption (A2)—that the F_{t+i} not be allowed to explode—is necessary. In its absence, the cost-minimizing decision for the firm is to set the discretionary component of effort, F, at a high and rising level. In such a case, the firm substitutes effort for current labor hours, but defers the repayment of this effort forever by continuously offsetting future increases in X with further increases in future F—a Ponzi scheme in effort. Any sensible implicit contract would forbid this.

The firm's choice of L_t will affect its choice of future L, and thus of the F_{t+i}. (Given L^*_{t+i} and X_{t+i}, F_{t+i} moves inversely with L_{t+i}.) The envelope theorem, however, guarantees that, if the F_{t+i} are chosen to minimize costs, then at the margin, changes in F_{t+i} will have no effect on C_t, since the F_{t+i} will be chosen so that at the margin they have no effect on C_{t+i}. Thus, in minimizing C_t, we can ignore the effects of L_t on the F_{t+i}.

Minimizing equation (2.34) with respect to L_t and multiplying through by L_t yields

(2.35)
$$\frac{dC_t}{dL_t} L_t = w_t L_t - \sum_{i=1}^{N} R^i w_{t+i} F_{t+1}^{-1} L^*_t y_i (1+\log F_t)$$

$$+ w_t \phi_0 J_t L^*_t - R w_{t+1} \phi_0 J_{t+i} L^*_{t+1} = 0.$$

Although for the sake of simplicity of notation symbols denoting expectations have been omitted, we should remember that equation (2.35) holds only in expectation.

Because E_t, J_t and J_{t+1} are all functions of L_t, a closed form solution for L_t will be messy indeed. Instead, the rate of change of labor hours is solved for by using a Taylor's series expansion around the log of lagged labor hours and implicit differentiation. The resulting equation is then linearized. Rather than burden the reader with the computations here, they are carried out in Appendix B.

The change in labor hours is given by

$$d \log L_t = \frac{Y+1}{Y+1+2\phi_0} d \log L*_t + \frac{\phi_0}{Y+1+2\phi_0} d \log L_{t-1}$$

(2.36)

$$+ \frac{\phi_0}{Y+1+2\phi_0} d \log_t L_{t+1} + \frac{Y}{Y+1+2\phi_0} d \log X_t,$$

where $Y = \sum_{i=1}^{N} y_i$ and dlogX means change in the logarithm of X. In particular, $\mathrm{dlog}L_{t-1} = \mathrm{log}L_{t-1} - \mathrm{log}L_{t-2}$, and $\mathrm{dlog}_t L_{t+1} = \mathrm{log}_t L_{t+1} - \mathrm{log}_{t-1} L_t$, where the subscript preceding L denotes the period in which expectations are taken. Labor hours behave as a weighted average of effective hours and lagged and expected future labor hours, with an added term depending on the "effort debt" being repaid by the firm. Other than this final term, equation (2.36) is a very standard result.[38]

Since L_{t+1} can be changed by the firm, equation (2.36) does not express the change in L_t solely as a function of variables which are exogenous to the firm at time t. Appendix B shows that equation (2.36) can be rewritten as

$$d \log L_t = q d \log L_{t-1} + \frac{(Y+1)q}{\phi_0} \sum_{i=0}^{N} d \log L*_{t+1} q^i$$

(2.37)

$$+ \frac{Yq}{\phi_0} d \log X_t + \frac{Yq}{\phi_0} \sum_{i=1}^{N} d \log X_{t+i} q^i,$$

where $q = \dfrac{Y+1+2\phi_0}{2\phi_0} - \dfrac{\sqrt{(Y+1+2\phi_0)^2/\phi_0^2 - 4}}{2}$.

In the case where L* is expected to be a random walk with drift, equation (2.37) becomes

$$d \log L_t = q d \log L_{t-1} + (1-q) d \log L*_t$$

(2.38)

$$+ \frac{Yq}{\phi_0} d \log X_t + \frac{Yq}{\phi_0} \sum_{i=1}^{N} d \log X_{t+i} q^i,$$

because $\mathrm{log}_t L*_{t+1} - \mathrm{log}_{t-1} L*_{t+i-1} = \mathrm{log}L*_t - \mathrm{log}L*_{t-1}$.

Because the X_{t+i} depend on L_t, equation (2.38) still does not express the change in L_t solely as a function of exogenous variables. Since effort, and thus effort debt X, increases with L*, the final term means a somewhat larger response of labor hours to a change in effective hours than the second right-hand side term of equation (2.38) alone implies. As we shall see in the next paragraph, however, q is small, so this effect is fairly unimportant.

We can now study the behavior of labor hours in response to a temporary or permanent shock to output. q is approximately equal to the share of marginal cost which is deferred, or $a/(1+a)$. For total manufacturing, we found that $a = 0.18$ (Table 2.1), meaning that $q = 0.15$. Thus, for manufacturing, 85%, or $1-q$, of the adjustment of actual labor hours to effective hours (and thus to output) takes place within the first year, while 13%, or $q(1-q)$, of the adjustment takes place within the second year, and the rest in later years. (The fact that discretionary effort returns so close to normal by the second year is the reason we earlier could make the simplifying assumption that the F_{t+i} in equation (2.35) equal unity.)

In addition, the adjustment which fails to take place in the first year causes an increase in X, effort debt, in following years, meaning that actual labor hours overshoot effective hours, before eventually settling to an equilibrium where the two are equal. (This theoretical finding is supported empirically by Nadiri and Rosen, who, using a reduced form model, find some overshooting of production worker employment and hours in manufacturing after four quarters.)[39]

In the case of a temporary shock (equation (2.36)), the overshooting of labor hours is larger. For example, consider an increase in output for one year, which is known to be temporary. Since the shock is known to be temporary, the firm knows it will incur adjustment costs when it discharges any extra workers it hires, so the initial change in labor hours is smaller than in the case where output is thought to be a random walk with drift. Since effort is thus higher, the change in effort debt X_{t+1} is larger than in the random walk case. In the next period, the return of output to its original level (or original trend) would cause labor hours to return to their original level if not for the effort debt and deferred marginal cost effects. These both push hours up, resulting in labor hours which are higher than effective hours for at least one period.

The overshooting of labor hours due to effort debt is very similar to Robert Gordon's end-of-expansion phenomenon. Gordon defined an end-of-expansion variable to be positive during the six quarters following the peak in the ratio of actual to potential GNP, and negative during the eight quarters thereafter. This variable has a significantly positive coefficient in a labor hours regression. Gordon interpreted this

Table 2.5
Gordon's End-of-Expansion Regressions, With Effort Debt Proxy

	1954:3-1977:4			1954:3-1985:4	
Constant	-2.43**	-2.44**	87.6**	-2.40**	92.6**
	(0.27)	(0.25)	(29.4)	(0.24)	(24.4)
1966-72 slowdown dummy[a]	0.61	0.61		0.59	
	(0.44)	(0.40)		(0.39)	
post-1972 slowdown dummy[a]	1.34**	1.35**		1.52**	
	(0.50)	(0.45)		(0.33)	
Current Q/Q*	0.48**	0.51**	0.49**	0.53**	0.51**
	(0.04)	(0.04)	(0.04)	(0.03)	(0.03)
Lagged Q/Q*					
One quarter	0.22**	0.22**	0.14**	0.19**	0.12**
	(0.05)	(0.04)	(0.05)	(0.03)	(0.04)
Two quarters	0.09	0.09*	0.05	0.07	0.03
	(0.05)	(0.04)	(0.04)	(0.03)	(0.03)
Three quarters	0.05	-0.00	-0.01	0.05	0.03
	(0.04)	(0.04)	(0.04)	(0.03)	(0.03)
Sum of Q/Q* coefficients	0.84	0.81	0.67	0.83	0.68
End-of-expansion effect		7.18**	5.63**	6.23**	4.69**
		(1.56)	(1.64)	(1.35)	(1.37)
Lagged L/Q			-47.4**		-50.1**
			(15.6)		(12.9)
Time			-0.44**		-0.47**
			(0.14)		(0.12)
1966-72 slowdown			0.23**		0.25**
			(0.07)		(0.06)
post-1972 slowdown			0.13		0.13*
			(0.08)		(0.05)
R^2	0.74	0.80	0.82	0.82	0.84
Durbin-Watson	1.67	2.02	1.92	1.93	1.85

[a] These variables have t statistics less than 0.25 when the time variables are added, so they were excluded from the two regressions which contain the effort debt proxy.
Notes: The dependent variable is the ratio of labor hours to potential output. Data are for the nonfarm business sector. Both the dependent variable and the Q/Q* variables are expressed as rates of change. * denotes significance at the 95% level. ** denotes significance at the 99% level. Figures in parentheses are standard errors.

as overhiring by firms at the end of an expansion, followed by a gradual dissipation of these workers.[40]

However, in the context of this chapter, we can view Gordon's variable as a proxy for lagged effort. Gordon simply captured the overshooting of labor hours described above. Since effort tends to be high during a rapid expansion of output, the peak in the ratio of actual to potential GNP will occur at or just after a time of high effort. Rapid expansion of labor hours after such a peak is thus nothing more than a repayment of effort.

Clear-cut proof of this hypothesis would require a clear-cut measure of effort—unfortunately, no such measure exists. Instead, I assume that deviations from trend in labor productivity are due to changes in effort. That is, low labor hours relative to output mean effort is high. If our hypothesis is correct, such effort will be repaid with extra hours (ceteris paribus) in the future. Thus, to Gordon's regression we add lagged labor hours per unit of output, expecting a negative sign. (High hours in the past mean effort was low, meaning higher effort now, and thus lower labor hours.) To deal with problems introduced by the time trend in this variable, we also add time to the regression.

The coefficient of lagged labor hours per unit of output is significantly negative, as expected (Table 2.5). In addition, its presence reduces the size as well as the statistical significance of the end-of-expansion variable, especially for the 1954-85 sample period. I conclude that a substantial part of Gordon's end-of-expansion phenomenon can be explained by repayment of deviations in effort from normal.

6. IMMEDIATE COMPENSATION FOR EFFORT

The contract discussed in Section 5 assumes that workers will remain with the firm long enough to be repaid for fluctuations in effort. But what about the case where turnover rates are high enough that workers may never be compensated for unusually high effort levels or that firms may never recoup the gift of low effort given in slack periods? In this section, we consider a contract in which workers agree ex ante to let effort vary with demand. There is no quid pro quo in which any realization of effort above or below the normal level will be precisely offset in the future, as there is in the contract discussed above.

Once again, I assume that output is produced using effective hours, the product of actual hours and effort. The firm and its workers agree to an implicit contract governing the relationship between labor hours and output. Output in turn depends on some observable economic variable beyond the control of the firm, such as aggregate demand. Since effort is a deterministic function of hours and output, it will also be a function of the observable variable.

The firm has two incentives to choose a contract which reduces the variability of labor hours (thus increasing the variability of effort). The first incentive was also present in the model of Section 5—to reduce the costs associated with adjusting labor hours, such as hiring and firing costs. The second incentive for reducing variability of hours is that utility-maximizing workers are willing to accept a lower wage in return for a contract which reduces the risk of being laid off. (In the first model, the wage was independent of the implicit contract.)

If these were the only factors governing the firm's choice of how much to let effort vary, the firm would offer a contract in which labor hours did not vary at all, with variations in output being met entirely through variations in effort, since there would be no cost offsetting the gains from increasing the variability of effort. In addition, however, the firm must compensate utility-maximizing workers for fluctuations in effort. In contrast with the model of Section 5, the workers or firm must be repaid for deviations in effort immediately. As long as the disutility of effort is convex, the firm will have to pay more when effort is high than it receives when effort is low, meaning that an increase in the variance of effort reduces expected profits. Thus, the firm chooses an equilibrium so that at the margin, the gains from increasing the variability of effort are offset by the losses.

To illustrate the implicit contract, I use a two-period model. In period 0, the firm is in a steady-state equilibrium with effective hours equal to actual hours. The firm has no information about period 1 other than that possible realizations of output, Y_1, are uniformly distributed between Y_0-H and Y_0+H. I assume that the contract governing the relationship between actual and effective labor hours takes the form

$$(2.39) \quad L_1 = bL*_1 +(1-b)L_0 ,$$

where $L*$ is effective labor hours and L is actual labor hours. Effective hours are proportional to output, $E(L*_1) = L_0$ and $E(L_1) = L_0$, where $E( )$ denotes expectations. When L_1 exceeds L_0, all period 1 workers are retained. When L_1 falls below L_0, layoffs are distributed randomly among period 0 workers. The firm sets b in order to maximize expected profits. The remainder of this section discusses the firm's profit maximization decision and its solution.

The firm's profits in period 1 are given by

$$(2.40) \qquad \pi = PY_1 - w_1 L_1 - a\left|L_1 - L_0\right| - g(F_1)L_1 ,$$

where P is price, which is assumed exogenous to the firm, w_1 is the period 1 wage excluding the cost of compensating workers for high effort, which is determined before the realization of Y_1 is known, and g is the cost per worker to the firm of compensating workers for above-average effort. g is thus a function of F_1, period 1 effort, which is defined as L^*_1/L_1, i.e., $F_1 L_1 = L^*_1$. L^*_1/L_0 is proportional to Y_1/Y_0. The third term on the right-hand side represents the cost of adjusting labor hours. I assume that any new workers hired in period 1 receive the same wage and compensation for extra effort as existing workers.

Thus, the firm's maximization problem is

$$\text{Max}_{b} E(\pi) = P\,E(Y_1) - E(w_1 L_1) - a\,E(\left|L_1 - L_0\right|)$$

$$(2.41) \qquad\qquad - E(g(F_1)L_1),$$

$$\text{s.t.} \quad F_1 L_1 = L^*_1.$$

The first order condition is

$$\frac{dE(\pi)}{db} = -\frac{dw_1}{db}E(L_1) - a\frac{dE(\left|L_1 - L_0\right|)}{db}$$

$$(2.42)$$

$$- \frac{dE(g(F_1)L_1)}{db} = 0.$$

In order to evaluate the derivative dw_1/db, I assume workers have utility proportional to income, so that utility equals w_1 if the worker is employed and 0 otherwise. The possible outcomes of output are assumed to be uniformly distributed between Y_0-H and Y_0+H. The probability of being employed (I assume that hours per worker do not vary and that all workers have an equal probability of layoff) in period 1 if employed in period 0 is 1 if $L_1 > L_0$ and L_1/L_0 otherwise. Thus, in cases where $L_1 < L_0$,

(2.43)
$$\frac{L_1}{L_0} = \frac{bL*_1 + (1-b)L_0}{L_0} = b\frac{L*_1}{L_0} + (1-b)$$

$$= b\frac{Y_1}{Y_0} + (1-b).$$

Since Y_1 is uniformly distributed,

(2.44)
$$E\left(\frac{L_1}{L_0}\right) = b\left[1 - 0.5\frac{H}{Y_0}\right] + (1-b)$$

$$= 1 - 0.5b\frac{H}{Y_0}$$

when $L_1 < L_0$ and 1 otherwise. Overall,

(2.45) $$E\left(\frac{L_1}{L_0}\right) = 1 - 0.25b\frac{H}{Y_0}.$$

In order to keep its workers, the firm must offer a contract providing expected utility U. Assuming the utility function of wages discussed above,

(2.46)
$$U = \left(1 - 0.25b\frac{H}{Y_0}\right)w_1 + \left(0.25b\frac{H}{Y_0}\right)0$$

$$= \left(1 - 0.25b\frac{H}{Y_0}\right)w_1.$$

Solving this equation for the wage, taking its derivative with respect to b and simplifying, we find that:

(2.47) $$\frac{dw_1}{db} = \frac{w_1}{\left(1 - 0.25b\dfrac{H}{Y_0}\right)}0.25\frac{H}{Y_0}.$$

Multiplied by $-E(L_1)$, this is the first term on the right-hand side of equation (2.42). The expected wage bill is thus raised by an increase in the variability of employment b because the firm must pay a higher wage to compensate workers for greater variability of employment.

To evaluate the second right-hand side term of equation (2.42), we must rewrite it:

$$(2.48) \quad -a\frac{dE(|L_1 - L_0|)}{db} = -a\frac{dE(|bL*_1 + (1-b)L_0 - L_0|)}{db}$$

$$= -aE(|L*_1 - L_0|).$$

Because $L*_1/L_0 = Y_1/Y_0$, this can be rewritten as:

$$(2.49) \quad -aE(|L*_1 - L_0|) = -aE(|Y_1 - Y_0|) = -0.5aH\frac{L_0}{Y_0}.$$

Thus, the second right-hand side term of equation (2.42) is negative—expected adjustment costs are increased, and thus expected profits are reduced, by an increase in b, the variability of employment.

In order to evaluate the final term of equation (2.42), I assume that

$$(2.50) \quad \begin{aligned} g(F_1) &= h(F_1 - 1) &\quad \text{when } F_1 > 1 \\ &= 0 &\quad \text{when } F_1 \leq 1, \end{aligned}$$

where $F_1 = L*_1/L_0$. Thus, when $F_1 > 1$,

$$(2.51) \quad \begin{aligned} g(F_1)L_1 &= h(L*_1 - L_1) \\ &= h(1-b)(L*_1 - L_0). \end{aligned}$$

Exploiting the proportionality of $L*_1 - L_0$ and $Y_1 - Y_0$, we find

$$(2.52) \quad \begin{aligned} \frac{d[g(F_1)L_1]}{db} &= -h\frac{L_0}{Y_0}E(Y_1 - Y_0) &\quad \text{when } Y_1 > Y_0 \\ &= 0 &\quad \text{otherwise.} \end{aligned}$$

Since $E(Y_1 - Y_0)$ conditional on $Y_1 > Y_0$ equals 0.5H,

$$(2.53) \quad \frac{d[g(F_1)L_1]}{db} = -0.25h\,H\frac{L_0}{Y_0}.$$

The final term of equation (2.42) is thus always positive. The firm's average cost of using effort is reduced, and expected profits are raised, by an increase in b because deviations in effort are reduced.

Using equations (2.47), (2.49) and (2.53), we can rewrite equation (2.42), the expression determining b, as

$$\frac{dE(\pi)}{db} = -0.25\frac{H}{Y_0}\frac{w_1 L_0}{\left(1-0.25b\frac{H}{Y_0}\right)} - 0.5aH\frac{L_0}{Y_0} + 0.25hH\frac{L_0}{Y_0}$$

(2.54)
$$= 0.5H\frac{L_0}{Y_0}\left[-0.5\frac{w_1}{(1-0.25b\,H/Y_0)} - a + 0.5h\right]$$

$= 0$ in equilibrium.

The firm thus sets b so that the incremental drops in the expected wage bill and in expected adjustment costs from reducing b are offset by the increase in expected effort costs. Since the first two right-hand side terms change sign when b falls below zero, b is constrained to be nonnegative. (It is the absolute value of b which determines the volatility of employment, so reducing b below zero increases volatility, increasing costs.) Since the second derivatives of the first term in equation (2.54) are negative and the second derivatives of the other terms are zero, the solution does indeed maximize profits.

While some of the implications of this model are similar to those of the earlier model, several are different. It is still true that procyclical productivity will follow from nominal shocks. However, we can no longer explain Gordon's end-of-expansion phenomenon.

7. CONCLUSION

This chapter has shown that a significant portion of the marginal cost of increasing output is deferred beyond the period in which output is increased. This has important implications both for measuring marginal cost and for understanding causality in the relationship between productivity and output over the business cycle.

By recognizing only current period changes in factor inputs as the marginal cost of changing output, Robert Hall introduced an upward bias into his measure of the markup of price over marginal cost. Taking account of deferred marginal costs significantly reduces the estimated markup. Labor costs are deferred by procyclical variations in effort. In the model of Section 5, workers are compensated with lower effort tomorrow in return for boosting effort today. The payback of this "effort debt" supplies an additional dynamic to the cyclical behavior of labor hours which helps explain Robert Gordon's end-of-expansion phenomenon.

Procyclical effort produces labor productivity growth which is also procyclical. Provided that demand shocks to the economy change desired output, they will also affect productivity. Such shocks can thus cause procyclical variations in productivity, a reversal of causality from real business cycle models in which variations in productivity lead to changes in output. The model of Section 5 shows that such a result is consistent with both profit maximization by firms and utility maximization by workers.

Taking account of deferred marginal costs also reverses Hall's finding that the marginal benefit of capital (price times marginal product per dollar rental cost) is negative. In fact, the marginal benefit of capital is positive and procyclical, varying between zero and one. One of the most intriguing results of the chapter is that in spite of this, firms act as if the marginal benefit of capital is always equal to one. An explanation for this phenomenon could provide some interesting insights into firms' pricing behavior.

APPENDIX A. WORKERS' UTILITY UNDER A VARYING-EFFORT CONTRACT

This appendix shows that, assuming the firm begins in steady state ($X = 1$, $L^*_{t-1} = L^*_{t-i}$ for all i), the implicit contract given by

$$(2.28) \quad X_t = 1 + 0.5 \sum_{i=1}^{N} y_i (1 + \log F_{t-i})^2 \frac{L^*_{t-i}}{L^*_t} - 0.5 \sum_{i=1}^{N} y_i \frac{L^*_{t-i}}{L^*_t}.$$

provides workers with at least as much utility as a constant-effort contract, assuming that:

(2A.1) workers' effort disutility is logarithmic in effort;
(2A.2) the firm agrees not to let the F_{t+i} explode (a Ponzi scheme); and

$$(2A.3) \quad \sum_{i=1}^{N} R^i y_i = 1.$$

I proceed by evaluating the discounted present value of worker utility under the two contracts as a Taylor's series expansion around $F_t = 1$, $L^*_t/L^*_{t+i} = 1$.

Let the expected present discounted value of the utility (negative disutility) of effort be given by

$$(2A.4) \quad V_t = -n E\left(\sum_{i=0}^{\infty} R^i \log E_{t+i} \right),$$

where E with subscripts denotes effort (as in the main text) and E( ) without subscripts denotes expectations. Since a constant effort contract would set all E_{t+i} to 1, the present discounted value of utility, V_t, under such a contract is zero. Substituting $F_{t+i} X_{t+i}^{-1}$ for E_{t+i} and equation (2.28) for X_t, we can rewrite equation (2A.4) as

$$V_t = -n E\left(\sum_{j=0}^{\infty} R^j \left[\log F_{t+j} - 0.5 \sum_{i=1}^{N} y_i (1 + \log F_{t+i-j})^2 \frac{L^*_{t+j-1}}{L^*_{t+j}} \right. \right.$$

(2A.5)

$$\left. \left. + 0.5 \sum_{i=1}^{N} y_i \frac{L^*_{t+j-i}}{L^*_{t+j}} \right] \right).$$

We will restrict the discussion to the effects on utility of changes in F_t and L^*_t/L^*_{t+T}, since changes in F_{t+i} affect utility in the same way as changes in F_t, while changes in L^*_{t+i}/L^*_{t+T+i} have similar effects on utility to changes in L^*_t/L^*_{t+T}.

I assume that the firm begins in steady state, so that all past F are 1 and all past L* are equal. In such a case,

$$V_t = \frac{\partial V_t}{\partial F_t}(F_t - 1) + \frac{\partial^2 V_t}{\partial F_t^2}\frac{(F_t - 1)^2}{2} + \frac{\partial V_t}{\partial\left(\frac{L^*_t}{L^*_{t+T}}\right)}\left(\frac{L^*_t}{L^*_{t+T}} - 1\right)$$

(2A.6)

$$+ \frac{\partial^2 V_t}{\partial\left(\frac{L^*_t}{L^*_{t+T}}\right)^2}\frac{\left(\frac{L^*_t}{L^*_{t+T}} - 1\right)^2}{2} + 2\frac{\partial^2 V_t}{\partial F_t\,\partial\left(\frac{L^*_t}{L^*_{t+T}}\right)}\frac{(F_t - 1)}{2}\left(\frac{L^*_t}{L^*_{t+T}} - 1\right),$$

where the derivatives are evaluated at $F_t = 1$ and $L^*_t/L^*_{t+T} = 1$.

The part of V_t which depends on F_t, called V'_t, is

$$(2A.7)\quad V'_t = -nE\left(\log F_t - 0.5\sum_{i=1}^{N} R^i y_i(1+\log F_t)^2\frac{L^*_t}{L^*_{t+i}}\right).$$

Taking the derivative of this with respect to F_t produces

$$\frac{\partial V_t}{\partial F_t} = -\frac{n}{F_t} + \frac{n}{F_t}E\left(\sum_{i=1}^{N} R^i y_i\frac{L^*_t}{L^*_{t+i}}\right)$$

(2A.8)

$$+ \frac{n}{F_t}E\left(\sum_{i=1}^{N} R^i y_i \log F_t\frac{L^*_t}{L^*_{t+i}}\right).$$

Setting F_t and the L^*_t/L^*_{t+i} equal to 1 and remembering (2A.3), we find that this derivative equals zero. Thus, the first order effect of a change in discretionary effort, F_t, is to leave workers' utility unchanged. Following the same procedure again, we find that $\partial^2 V_t / \partial F_t^2$ evaluated at $F_t = L^*_t/L^*_{t+i} = 1$ is n. This means that the second right-hand side term in equation (2A.6) is unambiguously positive, becoming larger the further F_t is from 1. Thus, the implicit contract given by (2.28) is structured so that both increases and reductions in discretionary effort raise worker utility.

The part of V_t which depends on L^*_t/L^*_{t+T}, called V''_t, is

$$(2A.9)\quad V''_t = 0.5nR^t y_T\,E\left(\frac{L^*_t}{L^*_{t+T}}\left[2\log F_t + (\log F_t)^2\right]\right).$$

This implies that

$$(2A.10) \quad \frac{\partial V_t}{\partial \left(\frac{L^*_t}{L^*_{t+T}}\right)} = nR^T y_T \left(\log F_t + 0.5(\log F_t)^2\right),$$

which is zero when evaluated at $F_t = 1$. In addition, it is obvious that $\partial^2 V_t / \partial (L^*_t / L^*_{t+T})^2$ is zero.

The remaining derivative, $\partial^2 V_t / (\partial F_t \partial (L^*_t / L^*_{t+T}))$, is equal to $nR^T y_t$ when evaluated at $F_t = 1$. Thus, the Taylor's series expansion of V_t under a varying-effort contract can be rewritten as

$$(2A.11) \quad V_t = n \frac{(F_t - 1)^2}{2} + nR^T y_T (F_t - 1) E\left(\frac{L^*_t}{L^*_{t+T}} - 1\right).$$

(This assumes future F_t and other L^*_{t+j-i} / L^*_{t+j} are held equal to 1.) The first term is positive any time discretionary effort deviates from the norm. If output follows a random walk, then $E(L^*_t / L^*_{t+T} - 1)$ is approximately zero, so the second term in (2A.11) is zero. If output fluctuates around a trend, then the second term will usually be positive, since discretionary effort, F, will tend to be high when output is above trend (and thus $E(L^*_t / L^*_{t+T})$ is greater than one) and low when output is below trend. Since the Taylor's series expansion of V_t is similar for L^*_{t+j-i} / L^*_{t+j} (for $j > i$) and for F_{t+1}, we have shown that, assuming the firm starts in steady state, a fluctuating effort contract of the form given by equation (2.28) will generally provide at least as much utility as a constant effort contract.

A worker who joins a firm which is owed effort by its workers, however, may find himself worse off under a contract where he must help repay this effort than under a constant effort contract. Workers will owe effort to the firm if discretionary effort has been low in the past. Mathematically, this corresponds to F_{t+j-i} which are less than one for some $j < i$. It can readily be seen from equation (2A.5) that such a case will reduce utility. To offset this loss in utility, the firm could offer higher pay, e.g., through a higher initial wage or through overtime work, or let the new hires work less hard than incumbents while the effort debt is paid off. If the firm raised wages, it would be compensated for the higher wages by the above-average effort of the new workers.

Even if a firm has been in steady state, new workers can be made worse off under the varying effort contract if the firm adopts a Ponzi scheme strategy. If the firm continually increases discretionary effort, offsetting the upward push of effort debt on hours with more and more discretionary effort, it never has to repay effort. Obviously, workers would not agree to the varying effort contract in such a case, so firms must agree not to let discretionary effort explode (assumption 2A.2).

APPENDIX B. LABOR HOURS UNDER A VARYING-EFFORT CONTRACT

The purpose of this appendix is to derive a formula for the log change in actual labor hours given equation (2.35):

$$\frac{dC_t}{dL_t} L_t = w_t L_t - \sum_{i=1}^{N} R^i w_{t+i} F_{t+i}^{-1} L^*_t y_i (1 + \log F_t)$$

(2.35)
$$+ w_t \phi_0 J_t L^*_t - R w_{t+1} \phi_0 J_{t+1} L^*_{t+1}$$

$$= 0.$$

Recall that even though symbols denoting expectations have been deleted for notational convenience, equation (2.35) holds only in expectation. To simplify the problem, I assume that the expected F_{t+i} equal unity. As the main text shows, our empirical results indicate that most of the labor hours adjustment for manufacturing takes place by the second year, meaning that $F_{t+i} = 1$ is a reasonable expectation. Incorporating equation (2.33), the assumption that the discounted real wage is the same in all periods, equation (2.35) becomes

$$\frac{dC_t}{dL_t} L_t = w_t L_t - \sum_{i=1}^{N} w_t L^*_t y_i (1 + \log F_t)$$

(2B.1)
$$+ w_t \phi_0 J_t L^*_t - w_t \phi_0 J_{t+1} L^*_{t+1}$$

$$= 0.$$

Because a closed form solution for the level of labor hours will be difficult, if not impossible, I solve for the rate of change of labor hours using a Taylor's series expansion around the logarithm of lagged hours. Excluding second and higher order terms, the general formula for the Taylor's series is:

(2B.2) $$\log L_t = \log L_{t-1} + \frac{\partial \log L_t}{\partial H_t} (H_t - H_{t-1}).$$

In our case, H_t is a vector of variables which includes $\log L^*_t$, $\log L_{t+1}$, $\log L_{t-1}$ and $\log X_t$. Technically, the derivatives are evaluated at $\log L_{t-1}$. Taking first differences, equation (2B.2) can be rewritten as

(2B.3)
$$d \log L_t = \frac{\partial \log L_t}{\partial \log L^*_t} d \log L^*_t + \frac{\partial \log L_t}{\partial \log L_{t-1}} d \log L_{t-1}$$
$$+ \frac{\partial \log L_t}{\partial \log L_{t+1}} d \log L_{t+1} + \frac{\partial \log L_t}{\partial \log X_t} d \log X_t$$

where dlog denotes "change in the logarithm of." In particular, $d\log L_{t-1} = \log L_{t-1} - \log L_{t-2}$ and $d\log L_{t+1} = \log L_{t+1} - \log_{t-1} L_t$.

In order to evaluate these derivatives, we use the method of implicit differentiation. Divide through equation (2B.1) by $w_t L^*_t$ and define the result as G_t:

(2B.4) $$G_t = \frac{L_t}{L^*_t} - \sum_{i=1}^{N} y_i (1 + \log F_i) + \phi_0 J_t - \phi_0 J_{t+1} \frac{L^*_{t+1}}{L^*_t} = 0.$$

This serves as our implicit function. To find $\partial L_t / \partial L^*_t$, we use the relationship

(2B.5) $$\frac{\partial L_t}{\partial L^*_t} = -\frac{(\partial G_t / \partial L^*_t)}{(\partial G_t / \partial L_t)}.$$

Since $\partial \log L_t / \partial \log L^*_t = (\partial L_t / \partial L^*_t)(L^*_t / L_t)$, we can multiply through equation (2.B5) by $L^*_t / \partial L_t$ to get

(2B.6) $$\frac{\partial \log L_t}{\partial \log L^*_t} = \frac{\partial L_t}{\partial L^*_t} \frac{L^*_t}{L_t} = -\frac{(\partial G_t / \partial L^*_t)}{(\partial G_t / \partial L_t)} \frac{L^*_t}{L_t}.$$

Using the same procedure:

(2B.7) $$\frac{\partial \log L_t}{\partial \log L_{t-1}} = \frac{\partial L_t}{\partial L_{t-1}} \frac{L_{t-1}}{L_t} = -\frac{(\partial G_t / \partial L_{t-1})}{(\partial G_t / \partial L_t)} \frac{L_{t-1}}{L_t},$$

(2B.8) $$\frac{\partial \log L_t}{\partial \log L_{t+1}} = \frac{\partial L_t}{\partial L_{t+1}} \frac{L_{t+1}}{L_t} = -\frac{(\partial G_t / \partial L_{t+1})}{(\partial G_t / \partial L_t)} \frac{L_{t+1}}{L_t},$$

(2B.9) $$\frac{\partial \log L_t}{\partial \log X_t} = \frac{\partial L_t}{\partial X_t} \frac{X_t}{L_t} = -\frac{(\partial G_t / \partial X_t)}{(\partial G_t / \partial L_t)} \frac{X_t}{L_t}.$$

The derivatives of G_t are straightforward to evaluate:

(2B.10) $\quad \dfrac{\partial G_t}{\partial L_t} L_t = \dfrac{L_t}{L^*_t} + \displaystyle\sum_{i=1}^{N} y_i + \phi_0 + \phi_0 \dfrac{L^*_{t+1}}{L^*_t},$

(2B.11) $\quad \dfrac{\partial G_t}{\partial L_{t-1}} L_{t-1} = -\phi_0,$

(2B.12) $\quad \dfrac{\partial G_t}{\partial L_{t+1}} L_{t+1} = -\phi_0 \dfrac{L^*_{t+1}}{L^*_t},$

(2B.13) $\quad \dfrac{\partial G_t}{\partial X_t} X_t = -\displaystyle\sum_{i=1}^{N} y_i,$

(2B.14) $\quad \dfrac{\partial G_t}{\partial L^*_t} L^*_t = -\dfrac{L_t}{L^*_t} - \displaystyle\sum_{i=1}^{N} y_i + \phi_0 J_{t+1} \dfrac{L^*_{t+1}}{L^*_t}.$

One other variable, $\log L^*_{t+1}$, could be included in H_t, the vector of variables in the Taylor's series representation of $\log L_t$. Using the same procedure as used for the other elements in H_t,

(2B.15) $\quad \dfrac{\partial G_t}{\partial L^*_{t+1}} L^*_{t+1} = -\phi_0 J_{t+1} \dfrac{L^*_{t+1}}{L^*_t}.$

Notice that this expression is identical to the negative of the final term in equation (2B.14). If we assume output, and thus effective hours, are random walks with drift ($d\log L^*_t = d\log L^*_{t+1}$), then these two terms will cancel in the expression for $d\log L_t$. Equation (2B.14) becomes

(2B.16) $\quad \dfrac{\partial G_t}{\partial L^*_t} L^*_t = -\dfrac{L_t}{L^*_t} - \displaystyle\sum_{i=1}^{N} y_i$

and we can ignore $d\log L^*_{t+1}$. Even if output is stationary around a trend, however, (2B.15) and the final term of (2B.14) are small enough to ignore: for annual data, $|J_{t+1}|$ is rarely greater than 0.1, and my estimate of ϕ_0 is considerably less than one.

Substituting the expressions given by equations (2B.10) through (2B.16) into equations (2B.6) through (2B.9) to find the derivatives contained in equation (2B.3), we obtain

(2B.17)
$$d \log L_t = \left(\frac{L_t}{L*_t} + \sum_{i=1}^{N} y_i \right) M_t^{-1} d \log L*_t + \phi_0 M_t^{-1} d \log L_{t-1}$$

$$+ \phi_0 \frac{L*_{t+1}}{L*_t} M_t^{-1} d \log L_{t+1} + \left(\sum_{i=1}^{N} y_i \right) M_t^{-1} d \log X_t$$

where

$$M_t = \frac{L_t}{L*_t} + \sum_{i=1}^{N} y_i + \phi_0 + \phi_0 \frac{L*_{t+1}}{L*_t}.$$

To be of use, equation (2B.17) requires a linear approximation. First, set expected $(L*_{t+1}/L*_t)$ equal to one, which should be nearly true (and exactly true if effective hours are a random walk). Secondly, although short run increasing returns to labor imply that changes in L_t will be smaller in absolute value than changes in $L*_t$, the levels of L_t and $L*_t$ will be very close, since changes in $L*_t$ are only a small fraction of the level of $L*_t$. Thus, we can also set $L_t/L*_t$ equal to one. To simplify notation, I define Y as

(2B.18) $\quad Y = \sum_{i=1}^{N} y_i .$

These linearizations allow us to approximate $d\log L_t$ as

(2.36)
$$d \log L_t = \frac{Y+1}{Y+1+2\phi_0} d \log L*_t + \frac{\phi_0}{Y+1+2\phi_0} d \log L_{t-1}$$

$$+ \frac{\phi_0}{Y+1+2\phi_0} d \log_t L_{t+1} + \frac{Y}{Y+1+2\phi_0} d \log X_t.$$

Since L_{t+1} can be changed by the firm, equation (2.36) does not express the change in L_t solely as a function of exogenous variables. Rewriting the change in labor hours terms using lag operators and using some algebraic manipulation, equation (2.36) becomes

(2B.19)
$$- \frac{\phi_0}{Y+1+2\phi_0} d \log L_{t-1} \left(1 - \frac{Y+1+2\phi_0}{\phi_0} L^{-1} + L^{-2} \right)$$

$$= \frac{Y+1}{Y+1+2\phi_0} d \log L*_t + \frac{Y}{Y+1+2\phi_0} d \log X_t.$$

Factoring the polynomial, equation (2B.19) becomes

$$-\frac{\phi_0}{Y+1+2\phi_0}\,\mathrm{d}\log L_{t-1}(1-QL^{-1})(1-qL^{-1})$$

(2B.20)

$$=\frac{Y+1}{Y+1+2\phi_0}\,\mathrm{d}\log L*_t+\frac{Y}{Y+1+2\phi_0}\,\mathrm{d}\log X_t.$$

where $\quad Q=\dfrac{Y+1+2\phi_0}{2\phi_0}+\dfrac{\sqrt{(Y+1+2\phi_0)^2/\phi_0^2-4}}{2}$

and $\quad q=\dfrac{Y+1+2\phi_0}{2\phi_0}-\dfrac{\sqrt{(Y+1+2\phi_0)^2/\phi_0^2-4}}{2}$

$$=1/Q.$$

Equation (2B.20) can be rearranged to form:

$$-q\,\mathrm{d}\log L_{t-1}(1-QL^{-1})=\frac{(Y+1)q}{\phi_0}\,\mathrm{d}\log L*_t\,(1-qL^{-1})^{-1}$$

(2B.21)

$$+\frac{Yq}{\phi_0}\,\mathrm{d}\log X_t(1-qL^{-1})^{-1}.$$

Since q is less than unity, the expressions containing L^{-1} can be replaced with infinite series, to obtain

$$\mathrm{d}\log L_t=q\,\mathrm{d}\log L_{t-1}+\frac{(Y+1)q}{\phi_0}\sum_{t=0}^{\infty}\mathrm{d}\log L*_{t+i}\,q^i$$

(2B.22)

$$+\frac{Yq}{\phi_0}\sum_{i=0}^{\infty}\mathrm{d}\log X_{t+i}q^i,$$

or

$$\mathrm{d}\log L_t=q\,\mathrm{d}\log L_{t-1}+\frac{(Y+1)q}{\phi_0}\sum_{i=0}^{\infty}\mathrm{d}\log L*_{t+i}\,q^i$$

(2.37)

$$+\frac{Yq}{\phi_0}\,\mathrm{d}\log X_t+\frac{Yq}{\phi_0}\sum_{i=1}^{\infty}\mathrm{d}\log X_{t+i}q^i,$$

where $\mathrm{dlog}L*_{t+i}=\log L*_{t+i}-\log_{t-1}L*_{t+i-1}$.

If L* is a random walk with drift, i.e., $\mathrm{dlog}L*_t=\mathrm{dlog}L*_{t+1}$, then, because $\dfrac{(Y+1)q}{\phi_0}\dfrac{1}{1-q}=1-q$, equation (2.37) becomes

$$\mathbf{d}\log L_t = q\mathbf{d}\log L_{t-1} + (1-q)\mathbf{d}\log L^*_t$$

(2.38)
$$+\frac{Yq}{\phi_0}\mathbf{d}\log X_t + \frac{Yq}{\phi_0}\sum_{i=1}^{\infty}\mathbf{d}\log X_{t+i}q^i.$$

NOTES

1. Observations of short run increasing returns to scale date back at least to Okun, 1962. For examples of industry studies, see Kuh, 1965; and Nordhaus, 1972. Cross-country studies include Brechling and O'Brien, 1967; and Gordon, 1986.

2. Shea, 1989.

3. Hall, 1986a, 1986b, 1986c, 1988.

4. Hall, 1986a, 1986b.

5. Hall, 1986c.

6. Hall, 1986a, 9.

7. Hall, 1986a.

8. Hall, 1986a.

9. Hall, 1986b, 290-91.

10. Hall, 1986a.

11. Hall, 1986c.

12. Hall, 1986a, 19.

13. Hall, 1986c.

14. Hall, 1986c, 24.

15. Hall, 1986c. The following discussion is from pages 12-13.

16. Hall, 1986c, 10-13.

17. Amemiya, 1977.

18. Hall, 1986c, 29.

19. Hall, 1986c, 23; Hall, 1986a, 21

20. Hall, 1986c, 23.

21. Hall and Jorgenson, 1967.

22. Epstein and Denny, 1980.

23. Okun, 1981.

24. Solow, 1972.

25. Akerlof, 1982, 545.

26. Akerlof, 1982, 551-52.

27. Akerlof, 1984, 81.

28. Hall, 1986c, 25.

29. Hall, 1986c, 26.

30. Hall, 1986a, 27.

31. Fay and Medoff, 1985, 648.

32. Shea, 1989.

33. Okun, 1962.

34. Fair, 1969.

35. Solow, 1968.

36. Kydland and Prescott, 1982.

37. Gordon, 1979.

38. For example, Clark, 1984.

39. Nadiri and Rosen, 1974.
40. Gordon, 1979.

III.

Simultaneity in Freely Estimated Production Functions

1. INTRODUCTION

The neoclassical theory of productivity growth, developed by Robert Solow and others, assumes a constant returns to scale production function in which technological change is independent of the inputs.[1] Some of the conclusions about long-run growth generated by this theory—that growth rates of output per worker across different countries should converge and that large differences in capital per worker across countries should result in large differences in rates of return and thus in large capital flows—appear inconsistent with empirical fact. More fundamentally, the basic assumptions of the theory mentioned above—constant returns to scale and the exogeneity of technological growth with respect to the inputs—have recently come under attack.

Paul Romer used several pieces of empirical evidence to argue that, in fact, technological growth is not exogenous, but endogenous, depending positively on the level of capital. In Romer's preferred specification for the production function, output is proportional to the capital stock while nearly independent of labor hours. One piece of evidence used by Romer to support this conclusion is a Cobb-Douglas production function freely estimated on low-frequency data.[2] ("Freely estimated" means the equation is estimated without a time trend. The logarithm of output is regressed on only a constant and the logarithms of each input.)

This chapter shows that any such freely estimated production function will ultimately fall victim to simultaneity. That is, (exogenous) productivity growth is the most important long run determinant of the relative costs of capital and labor, which in turn determine the capital-labor ratio. Strong productivity growth will thus boost both capital and output, creating the illusion of a causal link from capital to output in the estimated equation.

To simplify the analysis, Solow originally assumed that output was produced according to the Cobb-Douglas production function:

(3.1) $Y = DK^a L^b$,

where Y is output, D is the level of technology, or multifactor productivity, K is the capital stock, and L is labor hours. Under constant returns to scale, the parameters a and b sum to one. The marginal product of capital, which equals $aD(K/L)^{a-1}$ under constant returns, will thus vary inversely with the capital-labor ratio. Countries with relatively low capital-labor ratios should therefore have relatively high rates of return on capital, and should thus attract capital. In the real world, however, capital does not necessarily flow from rich to poor countries. Indeed, the U.S. was a net recipient of capital throughout most of the 1980s.

The neoclassical model also shows that, assuming constant depreciation and savings rates, as the capital stock, and thus total depreciation, grow relative to output, growth of the capital-output ratio will gradually slow until a steady-state growth path is reached along which output and capital grow at the same rate. This steady state rate of growth will depend only on the rate of technological change, and not on the savings rate. Assuming pure scientific knowledge is a public good, the rate of technological progress will be the same across countries, so steady state rates of growth will also be the same. Prior to reaching steady state, countries with higher capital-labor ratios (or higher output-labor ratios) should have lower rates of growth, causing eventual "convergence" of the output-labor ratio across countries.

The evidence on convergence is mixed. Edward Wolff found that for seven OECD countries, there is a strong negative correlation between the initial state of technology and subsequent capital-labor growth, thus implying convergence of growth rates.[3] Similarly, Baumol, Blackman and Wolff found strong evidence of convergence among a larger group of countries.[4] Romer, on the other hand, found that when an even larger group of countries was studied, there seems to be no relationship between initial levels and subsequent rates of growth of GNP per capita.[6] Baily and Schultze concluded that, in general, a large subset of nonsocialist countries are converging, but that other countries are not.[7]

Such questions about the empirical implications of the neoclassical model in turn raise questions about its key assumptions—constant returns to scale and the exogeneity of technological change with respect to the inputs to production. Either increasing returns or dependence of the level of technology on the size of the capital stock would be sufficient to explain nonconvergence of growth rates across countries and the lack of difference in rates of return on capital across countries. This chapter addresses one technique used to argue that the level of technology depends entirely on the capital stock—freely estimated production functions.

Paul Romer provided several pieces of empirical evidence that capital's coefficient in the production function is close to one and that labor's coefficient is close to zero. First, using the seven twenty-year intervals from 1839 to 1979 as data points, he found that growth of output per hour is inversely correlated with the growth rate of the labor force. If multifactor productivity is independent of labor hours, however, the two growth rates should be uncorrelated. Secondly, using both decade data from the 1850s to the 1970s and annual postwar data, Romer found that in a Cobb-Douglas production function freely estimated in log levels, the coefficient of the log of capital equals one while the coefficient of the log of labor hours equals zero. The only way to get estimated coefficients for capital and labor to resemble their revenue shares is to use differenced data.[7]

As further proof that labor's coefficient is zero, Romer showed that growth rates of output per hour and total hours are more negatively correlated than expected both across countries and across different sectors of the U.S. economy. In a regression of the growth of the logarithm of output on the growth in the logarithms of capital and labor for 16 countries over 30-40 year intervals (18 observations), Romer again found the coefficient on capital close to one and the coefficient on labor close to zero.

Although in a later paper Romer backed away from this view that capital alone matters, he did not challenge any of the earlier empirical evidence.[8] If indeed Romer's 1987 view is correct, the implications, two of which he cited, are profound. First, if labor receives a coefficient of zero in the production function, then policies which restrict employment in order to keep wages high have no adverse effect on output as long as they do not reduce capital formation. Secondly, the fact that capital's share of compensation is small relative to its contribution to value added implies that the private rate of return on investment is much smaller than the public rate of return. Investment thus has significant positive externalities. Romer argued that because investment, not savings, will thus determine national wealth, it is to a country's advantage to become a net foreign debtor, as long as the debt goes to build up its capital stock.[9]

This chapter argues that freely estimated production functions cannot be used to measure the underlying coefficients of capital and labor, due to simultaneity between the level of technology and the capital stock. If productivity growth in the general economy mirrors productivity growth in the capital goods-producing sector, then productivity growth will become embodied in the relative prices of capital and labor, which in turn determine the relative amounts of capital and labor employed. High levels of multifactor productivity in the economy, and thus in the capital goods-producing sector, will cut the price of capital goods relative to labor hours, inducing a larger capital stock at the same time that the high productivity is boosting output. Capital's coefficient in the production function will be biased upward as an estimate of its marginal product.

In addition, Section 2 shows that if relative factor input prices are included in Romer's regression, then the estimated coefficients on labor hours and capital should correspond to those of the underlying technology, assuming constant returns to scale. In the case of decreasing returns to scale, the estimated coefficients on labor and capital will not equal the actual coefficients, but will still sum to unity. Only capital's coefficient will be correct. Increasing returns to scale are ruled out because of the assumption of competitive goods markets.

Section 3 presents the empirical results from implementing the tests suggested in Section 2 using annual postwar U.S. data. Using several specifications for both expected inflation and the rate of return in the rental cost of capital, I find the reverse of Romer's results: capital has a coefficient of zero while labor has a coefficient slightly larger than one. The finding that the sum of coefficients on the two inputs is significantly greater than one, however, contradicts the theoretical results. When the constraint that the sum of coefficients equal unity is imposed, the coefficient on capital is positive, but still much smaller than its ex post revenue share. Section 4 discusses these results in light of the debate on the role of capital in productivity growth.

2. THEORY

My goal in this section is to replace multifactor productivity in the simple Cobb-Douglas production function with functions of inputs and relative input prices, in order to produce estimable equations for output which do not depend on time trends. In the first case, with multifactor productivity in the production function, output is simply proportional to capital times the ratio of the rental cost of capital to output prices. When the ratio of rental cost to output price is fairly stable, this is similar to Romer's result that output is proportional to capital. In the second case, with relative factor prices capturing all movements in multifactor productivity, capital's coefficient is "a", rather than one.

I assume all output is produced by two sectors: a consumption goods-producing sector, with Cobb-Douglas production function

$$(3.2) \qquad Y_t = D_{yt} K_{yt}^{a_y} L_{yt}^{b_y},$$

and a capital goods-producing sector, which has Cobb-Douglas production function

$$(3.3) \qquad X_t = D_{xt} K_{xt}^{a_x} L_{xt}^{b_x}.$$

At this stage in the development of the model, I allow for different Cobb-Douglas coefficients (the a_i and b_i) in the two sectors.

I assume there are always n firms in each sector. For simplicity of notation, the analysis is performed at the level of the firm. To get economy-wide values for output, capital or labor, one can simply multiply by n. Total capital, K_t, is $K_{yt}+K_{xt}$, while total labor, L_t, equals $L_{yt}+L_{xt}$. The total capital stock is determined by the relation

$$(3.4) \qquad K_t = (1-d)K_{t-1} + X_{t-1} + M_{t-1},$$

where d is the rate of depreciation and M is net imports of capital goods. (Net imports of capital goods do not affect the model, but must be taken account of when calculating the price of domestically produced capital goods.) Capital and labor are assumed to be mobile between sectors.

Both output-producing sectors of the economy are competitive. Y_t is sold to consumers at price p_{yt}. A competitive capital-renting sector buys the output of the capital-producing industry at price p_{xt} and rents it out to both the capital-producing and consumption goods-producing sectors at rental rate r_t. According to Hall and Jorgenson, the zero profit condition means that the rental rate must satisfy the following relationship:

$$(3.5) \quad P_{xt} = \int_t^s e^{\int_t^s (i_v - \pi_v)dv} \left[e^{-d(s-t)}(1-u_s)r_s \right.$$

$$\left. + u_s P_{xt} D_t (s-t)(1-q_s k_t) \right] ds + k_t P_{xt},$$

where i is the nominal cost of funds, π is the expected rate of inflation, u is the statutory (i.e., marginal) corporate income tax rate, $D_t(s-t)$ is the depreciation allowance per dollar of initial investment at time t on an asset of age s–t, k is the rate of investment tax credit, and q is the reduction in the depreciable basis of the asset as a proportion of the investment tax credit.[10]

The profit-maximizing conditions for the consumer goods-producing sector are:

$$(3.6) \quad b_y p_{yt} Y_t = w_t L_{yt}$$

and

$$(3.7) \quad a_y p_{yt} Y_t = r_t K_{yt}.$$

Similarly, the profit-maximizing conditions for the capital-producing sector are:

$$(3.8) \quad b_x p_{xt} X_t = w_t L_{xt}$$

and

$$(3.9) \quad a_x p_{xt} X_t = r_t K_{xt}.$$

Because of the assumption that goods markets are competitive, firms will be unprofitable if either of the sums $a_y + b_y$ or $a_x + b_x$ are greater than one. I am thus implicitly assuming that either constant or decreasing returns to scale prevails in both goods-producing sectors. The assumption of competition is necessary to derive a tractable solution to the profit maximization problem in the capital goods-producing sector. In order to simplify notation and to facilitate aggregation of the two sectors, I also assume $a_y = a_x$ and $b_y = b_x$.

Rewriting equation (3.2) as a function of labor hours, and substituting for capital from equation (3.7), we can write the demand for labor as:

$$(3.10) \quad L_{yt} = Y_t^{(1-a)/b} D_{yt}^{-1/b} \left(\frac{r_t}{p_{yt}} \right)^{a/b} a^{-a/b}.$$

Similarly, demand for labor in the capital goods sector is

$$(3.11) \quad L_{xt} = X_t^{(1-a)/b} D_{xt}^{-1/b} \left(\frac{r_t}{p_{xt}} \right)^{a/b} a^{-a/b}.$$

Under constant returns to scale, $1-a = b$, so labor is proportional to output, and varies inversely with the relative rental cost of capital.

Substitution of this expression for labor hours into equation (3.6), coupled with further algebraic manipulation, produces an expression for prices:

$$(3.12) \quad p_{yt} = w_t^{1-a} r_t^a L_{yt}^{1-a-b} D_{yt}^{-1} b^{a-1} a^{-a}.$$

Similarly,

$$(3.13) \quad p_{xt} = w_t^{1-a} r_t^a L_{xt}^{1-a-b} D_{xt}^{-1} b^{a-1} a^{-a}.$$

Prices are homogeneous of degree one in wages and the rental cost of capital. In the case of decreasing returns, an increase in the inputs leads to less efficient levels of production (assuming that the number of firms is constant), thus raising output prices for a given level of input prices. An exogenous improvement in productivity, i.e., an increase in D, will always lead to a drop in prices. If the production technology exhibits constant returns to scale, i.e., $1-a-b = 0$, and productivity grows at the same rate in the two sectors, i.e., D_{yt} is proportional to D_{xt}, then prices will grow at the same rate in the two sectors, i.e., p_{yt} will be proportional to p_{xt}.

One way to reexpress output so that it does not depend on the unobservable technology parameter is to simply rewrite the first order conditions (3.7) and (3.9):

(3.14) $Y_t = a^{-1} K_{yt} \dfrac{r_t}{p_{yt}}$,

(3.15) $X_t = a^{-1} K_{xt} \dfrac{r_t}{p_{xt}}$.

Output is proportional to the capital stock times the rental cost of capital divided by the output price. Defining the aggregate output price as

$$p_t = \frac{p_{yt} Y_t + p_{xt} X_t}{Y_t + X_t},$$

a similar expression for aggregate output can be derived:

(3.16) $Y_t + X_t = a^{-1} K_t \dfrac{r_t}{p_t}$.

Romer's empirical result that output is proportional to the capital stock stems from equation (3.16). Because movements in the capital stock dwarf movements in the real rental cost of capital (the logarithm of capital has a standard deviation roughly nine times as large as that of the log of the real rental cost over the period 1954-87), a regression of log output on log capital and log labor should produce a coefficient of one on capital and zero on labor. The crucial assumption driving this result is that productivity growth in the capital goods sector is the same as that in the consumer goods sector. Productivity growth is embodied both in declines in the cost of capital (r_t) and in declines in the price of output (p_t). The same productivity gain which lowers the relative cost of capital, increasing its usage, also increases output.

The importance of productivity growth in contributing to near-proportionality between output and capital can be seen by the failure of an analogous argument for proportionality between output and labor hours. In the same way that equation (3.16) was derived, an equation relating output to labor hours can also be derived:

(3.17) $Y_t + X_t = a^{-1} L_t \dfrac{w_t}{p_t}$.

As long as productivity fails to grow, output will be proportional to labor hours. It should be obvious from equations (3.12) and (3.13), however, that an increase in the D_{it} will cause a proportional increase in the w_t/p_{it}, assuming that the r_t/p_{it} are constant. (In steady state, this condition holds exactly.) Thus, whereas in equation (3.16) higher productivity is reflected in a higher capital stock, in equation (3.17) it is reflected in a higher real wage, w_t/p_t. Essentially, Romer found coefficients of zero on labor and one on capital because assuming that productivity grows at the same rate in the consumer and capital goods-producing sectors (constant r_t/p_t) is much closer to reality than assuming no productivity growth in either sector (constant w_t/p_t).

To this point, I have shown that a regression of output on capital and labor will not generate the underlying production function, but instead will show output roughly proportional to capital. In order to estimate the underlying production function correctly, we must reexpress the state of technology, D, entirely in terms of observable variables and constants. This can be done by rewriting equations (3.12) and (3.13) as

$$(3.18) \quad D_{yt} = \left(\frac{w_t}{p_{yt}}\right)^{1-a} \left(\frac{r_t}{p_{yt}}\right)^a L_{yt}^{1-a-b} b^{a-1} a^{-a}$$

and

$$(3.19) \quad D_{xt} = \left(\frac{w_t}{p_{xt}}\right)^{1-a} \left(\frac{r_t}{p_{xt}}\right)^a L_{xt}^{1-a-b} b^{a-1} a^{-a}.$$

For both sectors, improvements in technology (higher D) will be captured by the ratios of output to input prices. The seemingly perverse result that, in the case of decreasing returns to scale, an increase in factor inputs (the L_{it}) raises multifactor productivity (D), comes from misreading causality in the equations—the D_{it} are exogenous with respect to the L_{it}. The D_{it} are also exogenous with respect to prices— equations (3.18) and (3.19) say that improved multifactor productivity will reduce output prices (p_{xt}, p_{yt}) relative to the wage. Observable factor prices can thus be used as proxies for the unobservable D_{it}.

Substituting these expressions for D into the production functions (equations (3.2) and (3.3)), and rearranging slightly, we obtain new equations for output in the two sectors:

$$(3.20) \quad Y_t = \left(\frac{w_t}{r_t}\right)^{1-a} \left(\frac{r_t}{p_{yt}}\right)^a K_{yt}^a L_{yt}^{1-a} b^{a-1} a^{-a}$$

and

$$(3.21) \quad X_t = \left(\frac{w_t}{r_t}\right)^{1-a} \left(\frac{r_t}{p_{xt}}\right) K_{xt}^{\ a} L_{xt}^{\ 1-a} b^{a-1} a^{-a}.$$

One interesting feature of these equations is that no matter what the actual coefficients on capital and labor are, the sum of the coefficients from an estimated equation should be unity. In the case of decreasing returns, the lost productivity resulting from larger quantities of inputs is reflected in the relative input prices.

Multiplying through equations (3.20) and (3.21) by prices and summing, we find

$$(3.22) \quad p_{yt}Y_t + p_{xt}X_t = \left(\frac{w_t}{r_t}\right)^{1-a} r_t \left(K_{yt}^{\ a} L_{yt}^{\ 1-a} + K_{xt}^{\ a} L_{xt}^{\ 1-a}\right) b^{a-1} a^{-a}.$$

Since, from equations (3.6), (3.7), (3.8), and (3.9) we know that $L_{xt}/K_{xt} = L_{yt}/K_{yt}$, equation (3.22) can be rewritten as

$$(3.23) \quad p_{yt}Y_t + p_{xt}X_t = \left(\frac{w_t}{r_t}\right)^{1-a} r_t K_t^{\ a} L_t^{\ 1-a} b^{a-1} a^{-a}.$$

Using the definition of the aggregate output price, p_t, and rearranging slightly, equation (3.23) becomes

$$(3.24) \quad Y_t + X_t = \left(\frac{w_t}{p_t}\right)^{1-a} \left(\frac{r_t}{p_t}\right)^a K_t^{\ a} L_t^{\ 1-a} b^{a-1} a^{-a}.$$

Equation (3.24), which represents production as a function of inputs and observable factor prices, can be used to estimate capital's contribution to production without relying on unobservable time trends. The relative price terms—in particular the real wage, which rises when productivity improves—proxy for multifactor productivity, D. The fact that higher real wages induce capital formation explains Romer's results—changes in productivity directly affect the desired capital stock, so a simple regression of output on capital and labor hours contains simultaneity.

3. EMPIRICAL RESULTS

Data

Data for output, labor and capital are the same as those used by Romer for the postwar U.S.—the indexes used by the BLS in constructing estimates of multifactor productivity for the private business sector. (Because capital asset prices and capital stock data are generally not simultaneously available for the other data sets used by Romer, I can only examine U.S. postwar data.) w is the index of compensation per hour in the private business sector. p is the implicit price deflator for GNP. This chapter assumes that the Cobb-Douglas coefficients a and b are constant over the sample period.

In the Hall-Jorgenson treatment of rental costs, firms assume that the tax structure in place when a capital asset is purchased will remain the same throughout its lifetime. Thus $u_s = u_t$ and $q_s = q_t$ for all $s \geq t$. In addition, the economy must be near steady state, so that $r_s = r_t$ and $i_s - \pi_s = i_t - \pi_t$ for all $s \geq t$. Making these substitutions and then solving equation (3.5) for r_t, they found that

$$(3.25) \quad r_t = p_{xt}(i_t - \pi_t + d)\frac{(1 - k_t - u_t z_t(1 - q_t k_t))}{1 - u_t} \, ,$$

where $z_t = \int_t^\infty e^{(i_t - \pi_t)(s-t)} D_t(s-t)ds.$[11] Some of my empirical tests relax the Hall-Jorgenson assumption about tax treatment.

The measure of r used for the private business sector is the weighted average of the r for five components of business fixed investment: three categories of producers' durable equipment (motor vehicles, business machines, and other), construction of public utilities, and construction of nonresidential buildings. Excluded were purchases of mining and drilling equipment, because information on the tax treatment of these was not readily available. To avoid movements in capital costs due solely to shifts in the composition of the capital stock, the different r for each type of capital were weighted by each type of capital's real share (1982 dollars) of total capital over the sample period 1954-87.

For producers' durable equipment and for public utility construction, i, the interest rate, is a weighted sum of the cost of equity and the after-tax cost of corporate debt. For buildings, r is a weighted sum of three pieces which use various combinations of the cost of equity, public and private debt for i. Expected inflation was calculated as a second-order Pascal distributed lag of the growth rate of the GNP deflator. As indicated below, lag length makes only a modest difference in the results. Since the expected inflation term captures capital gains for the capital-renting firm, I am implicitly assuming that the expected price appreciation of capital goods (their capital gains) equals expected overall inflation.

In calculating the output price of domestically produced capital, p_x, to be used in equation (3.25) to calculate r, all construction is assumed to be domestically produced. The price for domestically produced business machines is set equal to the ratio of the sum of nominal purchases of business machines plus net exports of business machines to the sum of real purchases plus real net exports. For producers' durable equipment excluding autos and business machines, the same procedure is followed. Because business purchases of motor vehicles are not broken out separately from other foreign trade in motor vehicles in the NIPA, it is assumed that the price received by domestic producers equals the price paid by domestic firms.

Empirical studies of productivity consistently find short run increasing returns to labor—in the short run, firms change labor hours less than proportionately to changes in output.[12] In the model of this chapter, this corresponds to output being temporarily inside or outside the production possibility frontier. To correct for these cyclical effects (ignored by Romer), which may be correlated with labor hours and would thus bias its coefficient, variables which are correlated with the difference between actual and potential output but are uncorrelated with either of the gross inputs should be added to the regressions. I used both the ratio of the M2 money supply to GNP and the change in the unemployment rate for males 35 to 44 years old (RU). The unemployment rate for this age group, rather than for the entire labor force, was chosen in order to remove secular trends in the composition and characteristics of the labor force, and thus in the aggregate unemployment rate. Over the course of the business cycle, as labor hours rise above their trend, output increases more than one-for-one, causing labor productivity to rise. Without any correction for the cycle, the coefficient on labor hours will be biased upward.

Table 3.1
Production Function Coefficients of Capital and Labor, Estimated
Without Relative Factor Price Effects

	1948-84		1954-87
Least Squares			
log L	-0.45	0.04	0.17
	(0.29)	(0.28)	(0.26)
log K	1.03	0.84	0.80
	(0.08)	(0.09)	(0.08)
RU-RU$_{-1}$			-0.016
			(0.007)
log (M2/GNP)			0.61
			(0.17)
Standard error[a]	0.054	0.048	0.022
Durbin-Watson	0.63	0.40	0.87
AR2 correction			
log L	1.07	1.05	0.72
	(0.14)	(0.13)	(0.11)
log K	0.61	0.51	0.37
	(0.13)	(0.10)	(0.07)
RU-RU$_{-1}$			-0.004
			(0.002)
log (M2/GNP)			0.33
			(0.05)
ρ_1	1.37	1.38	1.24
	(0.17)	(0.19)	(0.19)
ρ_2	-0.41	-0.43	-0.29
	(0.18)	(0.19)	(0.19)
Standard error[a]	0.019	0.016	0.009
Durbin-Watson	2.00	1.99	2.05

[a] Standard error of the regression
Notes: The dependent variable is log(X+Y). Variables are described in the text. RU$_{-1}$ is the lagged value of RU. The equations also included a constant, whose coefficients are not reported here. The regressions were estimated using annual data. Figures in parentheses are standard errors.

Regression Results

Table 3.1 shows the results of the simple regression of log output on log labor and log capital for both Romer's 1948-84 sample period and this chapter's 1954-87 sample period. As one would expect, since we use similar data, my results for the 1948-84 sample period are very similar to Romer's. (I begin in 1954 because some information on the tax treatment of capital assets is not readily available for the earlier period.) Although the coefficient on labor hours differs substantially between the two samples, the results are qualitatively similar, and consistent with Romer's findings: capital's coefficient is insignificantly different from one, while the coefficient on labor hours is insignificantly different from zero. Surprisingly, the inclusion of the cyclical variables increases labor's coefficient. This is apparently an anomaly, however, since in all further regressions discussed in this section, correction for the business cycle reduces labor's coefficient.

Introducing an AR2 correction produces a radical but implausible change in the coefficients. In the two regressions which do not include cyclical variables to control for correlation between the inputs and the error term, the coefficient on labor hours, rather than being negative or zero, now exceeds one, even though the coefficient of capital remains implausibly high. Consequently, the sums of the coefficients on capital and labor, 1.68 and 1.56 in the two cases, suggest an absurdly high degree of increasing returns. Adding the cyclical variables produces more reasonable results. In fact, the shares of labor and capital are close to their shares of GNP.

In light of Romer's general line of argument, the justification for using an AR2 correction is tenuous. By regressing output on labor and capital, and nothing else, he is attempting to attribute all movements in output solely to these two inputs. The AR2 correction, however, by definition will attribute part of the current deviation in output from its fitted value to past deviations of output from past fitted values. The goal of freely estimating the production function is thus partly circumvented.

Inclusion of relative factor prices dramatically alters the results again (Table 3.2). For each measure of expected inflation, the estimated coefficient of log labor, b, is now greater than one. The estimated coefficient on log capital, a, lies in the implausible −0.06 to −0.01 range in each case. In spite of this, F-tests indicate that the sum of the coefficients of labor and capital is significantly greater than one, contradicting the theoretical result obtained in the previous section. I think this is caused by the failure of the cyclical variables to fully capture short-run increasing returns. In addition, variations in capacity utilization are not accounted for in the regressions. (When capacity utilization in manufacturing is added to the list of independent variables, its coefficient generally has the wrong sign.)

Table 3.2
Production Function Coefficients of Capital and Labor, Estimated
With Relative Factor Price Effects

	Mean Lag of Response of Expected Inflation to Actual Inflation, in Quarters			
Unconstrained	3	4	8	16
b	1.12	1.13	1.16	1.10
	(0.02)	(0.02)	(0.03)	(0.02)
a	-0.03	-0.04	-0.06	-0.01
	(0.01)	(0.02)	(0.03)	(0.02)
Standard error[a]	0.008	0.008	0.008	0.009
Durbin-Watson	1.97	2.01	2.07	2.05
Constraint: b=1-a				
b	0.98	0.97	0.98	0.89
	(0.05)	(0.07)	(0.11)	(0.06)
a	0.02	0.03	0.02	0.11
	(0.05)	(0.07)	(0.11)	(0.06)
Standard error[a]	0.028	0.028	0.028	0.027
Durbin-Watson	0.23	0.23	0.20	0.28
Constraint: b=1-a, with AR2 correction				
b	1.08	1.10	1.09	1.02
	(0.03)	(0.04)	(0.05)	(0.04)
a	-0.08	-0.10	-0.09	-0.02
	(0.03)	(0.04)	(0.05)	(0.04)
ρ_1	0.74	0.67	0.62	0.59
	(0.19)	(0.19)	(0.18)	(0.18)
ρ_2	0.24	0.31	0.36	0.38
	(0.20)	(0.19)	(0.18)	(0.18)
Standard error[a]	0.010	0.010	0.011	0.011
Durbin-Watson	2.08	2.09	2.10	2.09

[a] Standard error of the regression
Notes: The dependent variable in the unconstrained case is $\log(X+Y)$. b is the coefficient of $\log(wL/p)$, while a is the coefficient of $\log(rK/p)$. In the constrained case, a is the coefficient of $\log(rK/wL)$ in a regression whose dependent variable is $\log(p(X+Y)/wL)$. Variables are described in the text. Each regression also included a constant, the change in the unemployment rate, $RU - RU_{-1}$, and the ratio of M2 to GNP. All regressions were estimated using annual data for the period 1954-87. Figures in parentheses are standard errors.

When a and b are constrained to sum to one, as indicated by the theory, b is less than one while a is positive, ranging from 0.02 to 0.11. These estimates for a, however, are still significantly less than

Table 3.3

Production Function Coefficients of Capital and Labor, Estimated
With Relative Factor Price Effects and Assuming Constant Tax
Treatment

		Constraint: b=1-a	
	No constraint	Least Squares	AR2 Correction
b	1.07	0.61	0.94
	(0.05)	(0.07)	(0.07)
a	0.02	0.39	0.06
	(0.05)	(0.07)	(0.06)
P_1			0.59
			(0.18)
P_2			0.38
			(0.19)
Standard error[a]	0.008	0.019	0.011
Durbin-Watson	2.02	0.72	2.09

[a] Standard error of the regression

Notes: The dependent variable in the unconstrained case is log(X+Y). b is the coefficient of log(wL/p), while a is the coefficient of log(rK/p). In the constrained case, a is the coefficient of log(rK/wL) in a regression whose dependent variable is log(p(X+Y)/wL). Variables are described in the text. Each regression also included a constant, the change in the unemployment rate, RU- RU$_{-1}$, and the ratio of M2 to GNP. All regressions were estimated using annual data for the period 1954-87. Figures in parentheses are standard errors.

capital's revenue share. In addition, an AR2 correction pushes the estimated coefficient of capital below zero again. We have thus gone from Romer's case, in which output is entirely dependent on capital, to the opposite extreme, in which output depends almost entirely on labor hours.

Implicitly, the Hall and Jorgenson framework assumes that when a capital asset is purchased, the firm expects the tax treatment in place at the time of purchase to remain in effect throughout the tax lifetime of the asset. At the other extreme, one can assume that firms view all deviations in tax policy and rates of return from their sample average values as temporary. In equation (3.25), this means that r/p_x is a constant, equal to its average value over the 1954-87 sample period.

In the unconstrained case, estimated b is still greater than one, although estimated a is now marginally positive. The results are quite different, however, when the coefficients on labor and capital are constrained to sum to one. The coefficients on labor and capital obtained from such a regression (Table 3.3) are now very close to those expected based on capital and labor's revenue shares—capital's coefficient is 0.39 while labor's is 0.61. This is consistent with the theory outlined in Section 2—when relative factor prices are added, capital is no longer a proxy for productivity, so its coefficient falls to a level more consistent with its revenue share. When an AR2 correction is made, however, capital's coefficient is again only marginally positive.

One can also test the theory presented in Section 2 by comparing the fitted values for multifactor productivity with the actual values as calculated by the BLS. To do this, I use an approximate aggregate form of equations (3.18) and (3.19), assuming constant returns to scale:

$$(3.26) \quad D_t = \left(\frac{w_t}{p_t}\right)^{1-a} \left(\frac{r_t}{p_t}\right)^a b^{a-1} a^{-a} + \text{cyclical effects}$$

The variables w, p, and r are defined in the text, while a is the fitted value from the regressions discussed above. Charts 3.1 through 3.4 show actual and fitted multifactor productivity for both the case in which expected inflation responds to actual inflation with a mean lag of 16 quarters and the case in which all deviations in tax policy and rates of return from their sample average values are viewed as temporary. In each case, fitted multifactor productivity follows a pattern similar to the actual. The simple correlations between fitted and actual productivity fall between 0.98 and 0.99. The paths are closer in the two non-AR2 cases, and are almost identical in the case where r/p_x is constant.

These results indicate that relative factor prices are indeed a good proxy for multifactor productivity. To the extent that the capital/labor ratio is sensitive to relative prices, failure to account for them will bias the coefficients of capital and labor in a regression like Romer's.

4. CONCLUSION

This chapter shows that freely estimated production functions cannot be used to test either of the two crucial assumptions of the neoclassical growth model: constant returns to scale or multifactor

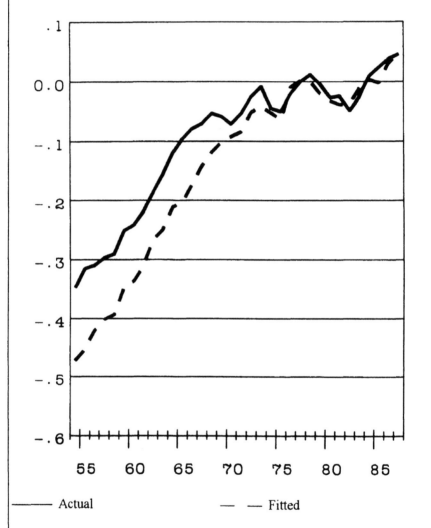

Chart 3.1
Actual and Fitted Values of Multifactor Productivity,
With No AR Correction
(Logarithms, 1977=1.0)

——— Actual   — — Fitted

Notes: Expected inflation is calculated as a second-order Pascal distributed lag
with a mean length of 16 quarters. Coefficients on capital and labor are
constrained to sum to one.

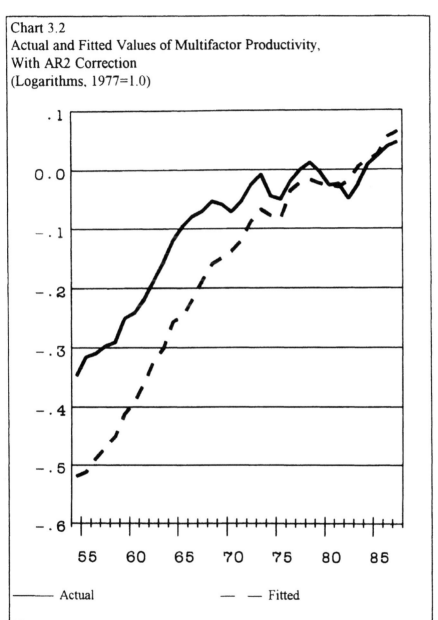

Chart 3.2
Actual and Fitted Values of Multifactor Productivity,
With AR2 Correction
(Logarithms, 1977=1.0)

———— Actual   — — Fitted

Notes: Expected inflation is calculated as a second-order Pascal distributed lag
with a mean length of 16 quarters. Coefficients on capital and labor are
constrained to sum to one.

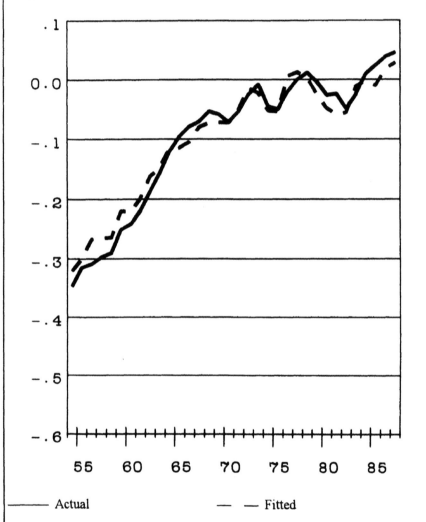

Chart 3.3
Actual and Fitted Values of Multifactor Productivity,
With No AR Correction, Assuming Constant Tax Treatment
(Logarithms, 1977=1.0)

————— Actual   — — Fitted

Notes: Firms assume tax law, interest rates and real rental rates will return to
their sample means. Coefficients on capital and labor are constrained to sum
to one.

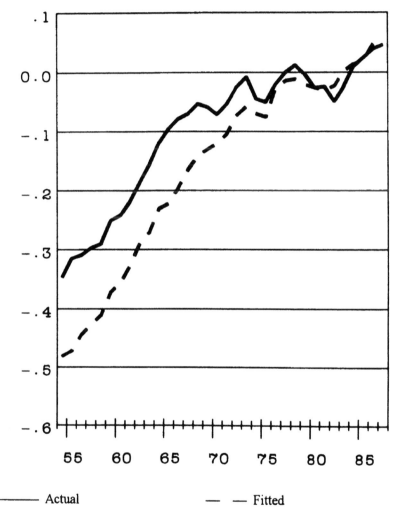

Chart 3.4
Actual and Fitted Values of Multifactor Productivity,
With AR2 Correction, Assuming Constant Tax Treatment
(Logarithms, 1977=1.0)

——— Actual   — — Fitted

Notes: Firms assume tax law, interest rates and real rental rates will return to their sample means. Coefficients on capital and labor are constrained to sum to one.

productivity's independence from the inputs to production. First, the estimated coefficients of capital and labor will sum to one whether the underlying technology is constant returns or not. Second, any regression of output on inputs alone will produce a coefficient on capital biased toward one and a coefficient on labor biased toward zero, no matter what the actual coefficients in the underlying technology. Recent work on the impact of capital formation on output growth, such as that of De Long, Summers, and Wolff, has emphasized the impact of investment rather than that of the capital stock,[13] and thus at least partially answers the criticism of this chapter.

Once the simultaneity between productivity and relative input prices is accounted for, the result that output depends primarily on the capital stock no longer holds. In fact, for postwar U.S. data, this chapter shows that inclusion of relative factor prices produces an opposite paradox—labor's estimated coefficient is close to one, while capital's is zero. These results probably stem from short-run increasing returns to labor and an inability to correct for variations in capacity utilization.

NOTES

1. Solow, 1956, 1960.
2. Romer, 1987.
3. Wolff, 1987.
4. Baumol, Blackman, and Wolff, 1989.
5. Romer, 1987, 62-66.
6. Baily and Schultze, 1990.
7. Romer, 1987.
8. Romer, 1990.
9. Romer, 1987, 69-70.
10. Hall and Jorgenson, 1971.
11. Ibid.
12. See Chapter 2, note 1.
13. For example, De Long and Summers, 1992; and Wolff, 1992.

Bibliography

CHAPTER 1

Akerlof, George A. "Gift Exchange and Efficiency-Wage Theory: Four Views." *American Economic Review* 74 (1984, no. 2): 79-83.

Allen, Stuart D., and Albert N. Link. "Declining Productivity Revisited: Secular Trends or Cyclical Losses?" *Economics Letters* 15 (1984): 289-93.

Amemiya, Takeshi. *Advanced Econometrics*. Cambridge, Ma.: Harvard University Press, 1985.

Blanchard, Olivier Jean, and Peter Diamond. "The Cyclical Behavior of the Gross Flows of U.S. Workers." *Brookings Papers on Economic Activity* (1990, no. 2): 85-143.

Clark, Peter K. "Productivity and Profits in the 1980s: Are They Really Improving?" *Brookings Papers on Economic Activity* (1984, no. 1): 133-81.

Cyert, Richard M., and James G. March. *A Behavioral Theory of the Firm*. Englewood Cliffs, N.J.: Prentice-Hall, 1963.

Davis, Steve, and John C. Haltiwanger. "Gross Job Creation and Destruction: Microeconomic Evidence and Macroeconomic Implications." *NBER Macroeconomics Annual* 5 (1991): 123-68.

Denison, Edward. *Accounting for Slower Economic Growth*. Washington, D.C.: The Brookings Institution, 1979.

Dickens, William T. "The Productivity Crisis: Secular or Cyclical?" *Economics Letters* 9 (1982, no. 1): 37-42.

Dickey, David A., and Wayne A. Fuller. "Likelihood Ratio Statistics for Autoregressive Time Series with a Unit Root." *Econometrica* 49 (July 1981, no. 4): 1057-72.

Fair, Ray C. "The Short Run Demand for Employment." Ph.D. diss., M.I.T., 1968.

Feldstein, Martin, and Lawrence Summers. "Is the Rate of Profit Falling?" *Brookings Papers on Economic Activity* (1977, no. 1): 211-27.

Gordon, Robert J. "The 'End-of-Expansion' Phenomenon in Short-Run Productivity Behavior." *Brookings Papers on Economic Activity* (1979, no. 2): 447-61.

―――. "The Jobless Recovery: Does It Signal a New Era of Productivity-led Growth?" *Brookings Papers on Economic Activity* (1993, no. 1): 271-306.

Griliches, Zvi. "R&D and the Productivity Slowdown." *American Economic Review* 70 (1980, no. 2): 343-48.

Hall, Robert. "Labor Demand, Labor Supply, and Employment Volatility." *NBER Macroeconomics Annual* 6 (1991): 17-47.

Hamermesh, Daniel S. "Plant Closings, Labor Demand and the Value of the Firm." NBER Working Paper No. 1839, 1986.

Kilby, Peter. "Organization and Productivity in Backward Economies." *Quarterly Journal of Economics* 76 (May 1962): 303-10.

Leibenstein, Harvey. *Beyond Economic Man*. Cambridge, Ma.: Harvard University Press, 1976.

Nelson, Richard R. "Research on Productivity Growth and Productivity Differences: Dead Ends and New Departures." *Journal of Economic Literature* 19 (1981): 1031-54.

Nordhaus, William D. "The Recent Productivity Slowdown." *Brookings Papers on Economic Activity* (1972, no. 3): 493-536.

Norsworthy, J. R., Michael J. Harper, and Kent Kunze. "The Slowdown in Productivity Growth: Analysis of Some Contributing Factors." *Brookings Papers on Economic Activity* (1979, no. 2): 387-432.

Pagano, M., and M. J. Hartley. "On Fitting Distributed Lag Models Subject to Polynomial Restrictions." Discussion Paper No. 356, Department of Economics, SUNY at Buffalo, 1975.

Perry, George L., and Charles L. Schultze. "Was This Recession Different? Are They All Different?" *Brookings Papers on Economic Activity* (1993, no. 1): 145-95.

Sachs, Jeffrey. "Real Wages and Unemployment in the OECD Countries." *Brookings Papers on Economic Activity* (1983, no. 1): 255-89.

Shapiro, Carl, and Joseph E. Stiglitz. "Equilibrium Unemployment as a Worker Discipline Device." *American Economic Review* 74 (1984, no. 3): 433-44.

Simon, Herbert A. "Theories of Decision-Making in Economics and Behavioral Science." *American Economic Review* 49 (1959): 253-83.

Sims, Christopher A. "Output and Labor Input in Manufacturing." *Brookings Papers on Economic Activity* (1974, no. 3): 695-735.

Smith, Adam. *The Wealth of Nations*. Cannan ed. New York: Random House, 1937.

Tobin, James. "A General Equilibrium Approach to Monetary Theory." *Journal of Money, Credit, and Banking* 1 (February 1969): 15-29.

Weisskopf, Thomas E., Samuel Bowles and David M. Gordon. "Hearts and Minds: A Social Model of U.S. Productivity Growth." *Brookings Papers on Economic Activity* (1983, no. 2): 381-450.

Williamson, Oliver. "A Model of Rational Managerial Behavior." In *A Behavioral Theory of the Firm*, edited by Richard M. Cyert and James G. March, 237-52. Englewood Cliffs, N.J.: Prentice-Hall, 1963.

————. *The Economics of Discretionary Behavior: Managerial Objectives in a Theory of the Firm*. Englewood Cliffs, N.J.: Prentice-Hall, 1964.

Yellen, Janet L. "Efficiency Wage Models of Unemployment." *American Economic Review* 74 (1984, no. 2): 200-205.

CHAPTER 2

Akerlof, George A. "Labor Contracts as Partial Gift Exchange." *Quarterly Journal of Economics* 97 (November 1982): 543-69.

————. "Gift Exchange and Efficiency-Wage Theory: Four Views." *American Economic Review* 74, no. 2 (1984): 79-83.

Amemiya, Takeshi. "The Maximum Likelihood and the Nonlinear Three-Stage Least Squares Estimator in the General Nonlinear Simultaneous Equation Model." *Econometrica* 45 (May 1977): 955-66.

Brechling, F.P.R., and P.O. O'Brien. "Short-Run Employment Functions in Manufacturing Industries: An International Comparison." *Review of Economics and Statistics* 49 (August 1967): 277-87.

Clark, Peter K. "Productivity and Profits in the 1980s: Are They Really Improving?" *Brookings Papers on Economic Activity* (1984, no. 1): 133-81.

Epstein, L., and M. Denny. "Endogenous Capital Utilization in a Short-Run Production Model." *Journal of Econometrics* 12 (1980): 189-207.

Fair, Ray. *The Short-Run Demand for Workers and Hours*. Amsterdam: North-Holland, 1969.

Fay, Jon A., and James L. Medoff. "Labor and Output Over the Business Cycle: Some Direct Evidence." *American Economic Review* 75 (September 1985): 638-55.

Gordon, Robert J. "The 'End-of-Expansion' Phenomenon in Short-Run Productivity Behavior." *Brookings Papers on Economic Activity* (1979, no. 2): 447-61.

————. "Productivity, Wages, and Prices Inside and Outside of Manufacturing in the U.S., Japan, and Europe." NBER Working Paper No. 2070, Nov. 1986.

Hall, Robert E. "The Relation Between Price and Marginal Cost in U.S. Industry." Manuscript, May 1986. (1986a)

————. "Market Structure and Macroeconomic Fluctuations." *Brookings Papers on Economic Activity* (1986, no. 2): 285-338. (1986b)

————. "Chronic Excess Capacity in U.S. Industry." NBER Working Paper No. 1973, July 1986. (1986c)

————. "The Relation between Price and Marginal Cost in U.S. Industry." *Journal of Political Economy* 96 (October 1988): 921-47.

Hall, Robert E., and Dale W. Jorgenson. "Tax Policy and Investment Behavior." *American Economic Review* 57 (June 1967): 391-414.

Kuh, Edwin. "Cyclical and Secular Labor Productivity in United States Manufacturing." *Review of Economics and Statistics* 47 (February 1965): 1-12.

Kydland, Finn E., and Edward C. Prescott. "Time to Build and Aggregate Fluctuations." *Econometrica* 50 (1982): 1345-70.

Nadiri, M. Ishaq, and Sherwin Rosen. *A Disequilibrium Model of Demand for Factors of Production*. New York: National Bureau of Economic Research, 1974.

Nordhaus, William D. "The Recent Productivity Slowdown." *Brookings Papers on Economic Activity* (1972, no. 3): 493-356.

Okun, Arthur M. "Potential GNP: Its Measurement and Significance." *American Statistical Association, Proceedings of the Business and Economics Section* (1962): 98-104.

————. *Prices and Quantities*. Washington, D.C.: The Brookings Institution, 1981.

Shea, John. "Labor Effort and the Business Cycle." Manuscript, May 1989.

Solow, Robert M. "Short-run Adjustment of Employment to Output." In *Value, Capital, and Growth: Papers in honour of Sir John Hicks*, edited by J. N. Wolfe. Aldine, 1968.

————. "Some Evidence on the Short-Run Productivity Puzzle." In *Development and Planning*, edited by Jagdish Bhagwati and Richard Eckaus. London: Allen and Unwin, 1972.

CHAPTER 3

Baily, Martin Neil and Charles L. Schultze. "The Productivity of Capital in a Period of Slower Growth." *Brookings Papers on Economic Activity: Microeconomics* (1990): 369-406.

Baumol, William J., Sue Anne Batey Blackman, and Edward N. Wolff. *Productivity and American Leadership: The Long View*. Cambridge, Mass.: MIT Press, 1989.

De Long, J. Bradford and Lawrence H. Summers. "Equipment Investment and Economic Growth: How Strong Is the Nexus?" *Brookings Papers on Economic Activity* (1992:2): 157-199.

Hall, Robert E. and Dale W. Jorgenson. "Application of the Theory of Optimum Capital Accumulation." In *Tax Incentives and Capital Spending*, edited by Gary Fromm. Washington, D.C.: The Brookings Institution, 1971.

Romer, Paul M. "Crazy Explanations for the Productivity Slowdown." Manuscript, March 1987.

————. "Capital, Labor, and Productivity." *Brookings Papers on Economic Activity: Microeconomics* (1990): 337-67.

Solow, Robert M. "A Contribution to the Theory of Economic Growth." *Quarterly Journal of Economics* 70 (February 1956): 65-94.

————. "Investment and Technical Progress." In *Mathematical Methods in the Social Sciences*, edited by Kenneth J. Arrow, Samuel Karlin and Patrick Suppes. Stanford University Press, 1960.

Wolff, Edward N. "Capital Formation and Long-Term Productivity Growth: A Comparison of Seven Countries." New York University: Economic Research Reports No. 87-37, September 1987.

————. "Capital Formation and Productivity Growth in the 1970s and 1980s: A Comparative Look at OECD Countries." In *Tools for American Workers: The Role of Machinery and Equipment In Economic Growth*, American Council for Capital Formation: Center for Policy Research, Washington, D.C., December 1992.

Index

For Product Safety Concerns and Information please contact our EU
representative GPSR@taylorandfrancis.com Taylor & Francis Verlag GmbH,
Kaufingerstraße 24, 80331 München, Germany

Batch number: 08158427

Printed by Printforce, the Netherlands